Bringing
Out the Best
in Teachers

THIRD EDITION

D0957899

To the teachers who participated in the study on which
this book is based, to the outstanding principals they described,
and to Dale and Evan for their patience.

THIRD EDITION

Bringing Out the Best in Teachers

What Effective Principals Do

Joseph Blase
Peggy C. Kirby

CORWIN PRESS

A SAGE Company
Thousand Oaks, CA 91320

For information:

 Corwin Press
A SAGE Company
2455 Teller Road
Thousand Oaks, California 91320
www.corwinpress.com

SAGE Ltd.
1 Oliver's Yard
55 City Road
London, EC1Y 1SP
United Kingdom

SAGE India Pvt. Ltd.
B 1/I 1 Mohan Cooperative
Industrial Area
Mathura Road, New Delhi 110 044
India

SAGE Asia-Pacific Pte. Ltd.
33 Pekin Street #02-01
Far East Square
Singapore 048763

Printed in the United States of America.

Library of Congress Cataloging-in-Publication Data

Blase, Joseph.
 Bringing out the best in teachers : what effective principals do /
Joseph Blase, Peggy C. Kirby. — 3rd ed.
  p. cm.
Includes bibliographical references and index.
ISBN 978-1-4129-6519-4 (cloth) — ISBN 978-1-4129-6520-0 (pbk.)
1. Teacher-principal relationships. I. Kirby, Peggy C. II. Title.

LB2840.B57 2009
371.2'012—dc22

2008020181

This book is printed on acid-free paper.

08 09 10 11 10 9 8 7 6 5 4 3 2 1

Acquisitions Editor:	Arnis Burvikovs
Associate Editor:	Desirée Enayati
Production Editor:	Appingo Publishing Services
Cover Designer:	Anthony Paular

Contents

Foreword to
the Third Edition

The school bell sounds at 9:00 a.m. at Estelle Elementary in Marrero, Louisiana. Serving 930 students pre-K through 5, Estelle sits in a working-class suburb across the Mississippi River from New Orleans. We enjoy a wonderful mix of ethnicities and family groups which range from two-parent homes to grandparents rearing grandchildren or even great-grandchildren, to father-only or mother-only homes, to foster families. In these trying post-Katrina times, many families still live in cramped FEMA trailers or with multiple family groups.

We at Estelle also have been entrusted with the most medically-fragile special needs students in our school district. As young as three years of age, our students with special needs give all of us the courage to face whatever challenges come our way. Who could complain when they see a child who is severely involved use a switch device to communicate a want for the first time? Or a child confined to a wheelchair laugh with glee as he dog-paddles unfettered across the therapy pool? The School Reflection Garden is a memorial to the 58 students who have passed on from this life over the last 20 years. Just today we lost another angel. Each student who has gone on to the next life is depicted as an angel on a ceramic tile that was hand painted by an Estelle student in the Talent Program. The tile has the names of the student who passed away as well as the student artist who created it. Our special children are gone but never to be forgotten.

Many of our students attend Estelle because their parents or grandparents attended Estelle. Our parents take pride in being involved in their children's school. We receive many requests from parents living outside of the attendance zone for their children to be given permits to attend Estelle.

What is the magnet that draws these families to want their children to attend Estelle? I believe that the pull, the natural draw, is that Estelle is an inviting, supportive, and nurturing learning environment. Our mission is simple: "Estelle = Educating Students to Experience Life-Long Excellence." Testimonials about the positive impact of our faculty and staff on the lives of Estelle students support our claim. Former students return to share their success stories: making the honor roll in middle or high school, receiving scholarships, or succeeding on the job.

The school bell sounds a familiar chime, for I have arrived at this school every morning for 20 years. I confess that this it not "just a job" for me. It is my passion. I am not a middle manager, as principals were considered when I first started the principalship. I am a leader, a transformational leader, who has the power to create a school climate that supports students, faculty, staff, parents, and the school community by my words, gestures, and deeds.

I start every day by telling our students that I love them. Parents are always welcome. Teachers know that I am here to remove any barriers that stand in their way of being the most effective teacher for their classes and teacher leaders for our school.

Support, assistance, and reinforcement is what is needed by both adults and children in the greater New Orleans area as we continue to struggle back from the physical and emotional destruction of Hurricanes Katrina and Rita. Two years later, many remain scarred. But our school is a sanctuary that I will protect.

The work of Blase and Kirby resonates clearly for me. Although I am a seasoned principal, it still serves as a gut check for principals struggling not just with a storm's aftermath and children with unimaginable challenges, but also with the taxing mandates of No Child Left Behind and its hallmark, high stakes tests, with a disillusioned profession, and an accusatory public. But we know that we must educate every child, regardless of the gifts or limitations the child brings to the public school. If I want our students to be successful, I must support our teachers in creating education that is meaningful and engaging.

Bringing Out the Best in Teachers: What Effective Principals Do gives teachers voice in identifying what they need to be successful. It provides relevant research in an easy-to-digest format. Blase and Kirby have given principals a gift, a means to assist us in getting a grip on priorities, especially for those who grasp school keys for the first time. The third edition provides a blueprint for principals. It is an excellent springboard for reflecting on our own strengths and challenges. Those aspiring to leadership roles are well-advised to read this book first. It takes the right personality and skill set to motivate heretofore unappreciated, underpaid, and overworked teachers. The third edition of *Bringing Out the Best in Teachers* validates the role of the principal—we are the shepherds who tend to the needs of teachers, bringing them together as a collegial, professional learning community.

We praise, we support, we expect, we empower, we suggest, we model, we care. The school bell sounds and we are ready.

Jackie H. Daniilidis
Estelle Elementary School, Principal
Jefferson Parish Public Schools
Marrero, LA

Preface to
the Third Edition

*Leaders aren't born, they are made—and they are made just like
anything else, through hard work.*

—Vincent Lombardi

This book is for school principals—both practicing and prospec-
tive—who want to bring out the best in teachers. It is intended to
help them examine, rather specifically, what they can do to influence
teachers and their performance. Unfortunately, the relationship
between school leadership and its effects on teachers and their work
has not been explored fully in the educational literature. This literature
tends to be quite abstract and often misses many of the important and
concrete elements that make up the everyday world of the school. The
practical and prescriptive literature is not adequately informed by solid
empirical research. Moreover, the simplistic recipes for effectiveness
that are typically offered offend practitioners who understand full well
the complex nature of school leadership, teaching, and learning. On
both counts, it is hoped that this book will be a relief.

Bringing Out the Best in Teachers is based on an in-depth study
of the everyday strategies that effective school principals use to
influence, motivate, and empower teachers. It is written entirely
from the teacher's perspective, a perspective that has largely been
ignored in the administration literature. The research approach used
to collect the data for this book allowed teachers to identify and
describe freely, in their own words and in great detail, how effective

principals influence them and exactly how such influence affects their teaching and, more generally, their work with students.

Here you will find detailed portrayals of what effective transformational principals actually do—from the teacher's point of view—that lead to improved teacher motivation, commitment, and innovation and enhance teachers' abilities to achieve high academic and social goals with students. The descriptions from the teachers' reports are presented in a straightforward and understandable way. We wrote this book on the premise that administrators have a better chance of developing meaningful ways of working with teachers if they take the opportunity to reflect critically on their leadership within the context of knowledge produced from a study of teachers' perspectives on effective leadership.

Many physical and psychological barriers make interaction and communication between administrators and teachers difficult. Teachers are physically and psychologically isolated from administrators; their desire for autonomy increases this isolation. Principals face overwhelming demands for their time, and their formal authority is limited. Teachers, therefore, may choose to disregard school principals whose goals and strategies of influence are inconsistent with school goals and teachers' professional norms and expectations. When teachers' and principals' purposes and strategies are incongruent, a climate is created that prevents them from reaping the benefits (such as elevated levels of teacher motivation and commitment) that effective leadership can have for them and, indirectly, for students.

What kinds of principal-teacher interaction do produce these benefits? The centerpiece of this book—Chapters 2 through 9—describes the strategies and related practices employed by effective principals to enhance teachers and their work with students. Principals' goals in using the strategies and the specific consequences for teachers are fully described. Each chapter closes with a set of guidelines for the reader's consideration.

In Chapter 1, we present a brief overview of research on the principalship and a description of the research methods employed. Chapters 2 and 3, respectively, focus on the importance of praise and how principals articulate expectations to effect changes in teacher thinking and behavior. In Chapter 4, we examine the many ways principals involve teachers in instructional and noninstructional decisions. Chapter 5 describes how, by extending autonomy to teachers, principals are able to enhance teachers' development. Several strategies—including the use of rewards and principal support—are discussed in Chapter 6. Indirect, subtle, and yet powerful strategies—including giving advice, providing opportunities for professional development, and distributing professional literature—are explored in Chapter 7. Chapter 8 considers the consequences of employing formal authority to ensure teacher compliance. In Chapter 9, the significance of three personality characteristics (consideration, optimism, and honesty) and two strategies (modeling and visibility) are highlighted. Chapter 10, the final chapter, challenges the reader to consider the applicability of the leadership strategies discussed herein for school restructuring.

This book discusses some fine, even extraordinary, principals whose dynamic leadership has had remarkably positive effects on teachers and, we suspect, on students as well. It describes these principals as seen through the eyes of teachers. The book shows what happens when school principals work to create open, honest, and sincere relationships with teachers. Principals who have studied and used the strategies discussed in this book tell us that they were able to create school environments that focus on the social and educational welfare of students and that such schools are possible because they bring out the best in teachers.

WHAT'S NEW IN THE THIRD EDITION

In this third edition we review additional relevant published literature, including effective school-based leadership, transformational leadership, school productivity and school effects, data analysis, and adult learning. We also compare findings about effective principal leadership to standards developed by the Interstate School Leaders Licensure Consortium (ISLLC) and the Educational Leaders Constituent Council (ELCC). In so doing, it is evident how timely the study that is the basis of this book remains.

Acknowledgments

We would like to express our special thanks to Professor Jo Blase—particularly for the authorship of Chapter 1 as well as for her assistance with editorial and academic matters.

PUBLISHER'S ACKNOWLEDGMENTS

Corwin Press gratefully acknowledges the contributions of the following reviewers:

Melody Aldrich, Teacher
Florence High School
Florence, AZ

Pam Newell Bradley, Principal
Irving Elementary School
Muskogee, OK

Denise Carlson, Curriculum Consultant
Heartland Area Education Agency
Johnston, IA

Carrie Clark, Teacher
Gilbert Elementary School
Gilbert, IA

Cynthia Martone, School Management Advisor
Zainab Girls Preparatory School
Doha, Qatar

Lyndon Oswald, Principal
Sandcreek Middle School
Idaho Falls, ID

Michele Pecina, Principal
Millview Elementary School
Madera, CA

David Raleigh, Assistant Principal
Frankfort High School
Frankfort, KY

Marilyn Steneken, Teacher
Sparta Middle School
Sparta, NJ

About the Authors

 **Joseph Blase** is a professor of educational administration at the University of Georgia. Since receiving his PhD in 1980 from Syracuse University, his research has focused on school reform, transformational leadership, the micropolitics of education, principal-teacher relationships, and the work lives of teachers. His work concentrating on school-level micropolitics received the 1988 Davis Memorial Award given by the University Council for Educational Administration, and his coauthored article published in the *Journal of Educational Administration* won the W. G. Walker 2000 Award for Excellence. In 1999 he was recognized as an elite scholar, one of the 50 Most Productive and Influential Scholars of Educational Administration in the world. Blase edited *The Politics of Life in Schools: Power, Conflict, and Cooperation* (winner of the 1994 Critic's Choice Award sponsored by the American Education Studies Association, Sage, 1991); coauthored, with Peggy Kirby, *Bringing Out the Best in Teachers* (1994, 2000); coauthored, with Gary Anderson, *The Micropolitics of Educational Leadership* (1995); and coauthored, with Jo Blase, *Empowering Teachers* (1994, 2000), *Handbook of Instructional Leadership* (1998, 2004), *Breaking the Silence* (2003), and *Teachers Bringing Out the Best in Teachers* (2006). Professor Blase has published over 120 academic articles, chapters, and books.

 **Peggy C. Kirby** is former Professor of Educational Leadership and Foundations and University Research Professor and Endowed Professor for School Improvement at the University of New Orleans, where she taught graduate courses in research and school leadership. She is a certified teacher and program evaluator in the state of Louisiana. Since receiving a PhD in educational administration in 1987, she investigated school-level factors, particularly leadership and governance, that influence student and teacher outcomes. She cofounded the Jefferson Community School, Louisiana's first charter school that serves middle school students at risk of failure due to chronic discipline problems. She coauthored, with Vincent Anfara, Jr., *Voices From the Middle: Decrying What Is, Imploring What Could Be* (1999). Her research publications have focused on alternative middle schools, shared leadership, ethics in educational administration, charter schools, and classroom processes related to effective schooling, and have appeared in journals such as the *American Journal of Education*, the *Journal of Educational Administration*, and the *Middle School Journal*.

Dr. Kirby is now President of *ed-cet, inc.*, an educational research, evaluation, and consulting firm based in New Orleans. Her clients include school districts in 12 states that received federal or state funds to improve instruction, leadership, and climate in their schools. She helped create the School Leadership Center of Greater New Orleans which emphasizes cross-district collegiality, professionalism, and research-based school improvement. Through it, she continues to assist school leaders in examining and implementing alternative forms of governance based on teacher empowerment.

CHAPTER ONE

Principals and Their Effectiveness

Transforming leadership recognizes and exploits an existing need or demand of a potential follower . . . looks for potential motives in followers, seeks to satisfy higher needs, and engages the full person of the follower. The result of transforming leadership is a relationship of mutual stimulation and elevation that converts followers into leaders and may convert leaders into moral agents.

—Burns, 1978, p. 4

Leadership is not magnetic personality—that can just as well be a glib tongue. It is not "making friends and influencing people"—that is flattery. Leadership is lifting a person's vision to high sights, the raising of a person's performance to a higher standard, the building of a personality beyond its normal limitations.

—Peter Drucker, 2001, ¶37

PRINCIPAL EFFECTIVENESS: A BRIEF HISTORICAL OVERVIEW

Both scholars and practitioners of educational administration believe that principals play a critical role in schools. Many argue that school

1

principals can affect virtually all aspects of school life. Yet, empirical research provides few detailed pictures of the everyday social and behavioral dynamics of effective school-based leadership. This is especially true with regard to understanding leadership from the perspective of teachers and, in particular, how school leadership enhances teachers and their overall performance. This book helps fill the gap by adding to the knowledge about how truly effective principals influence teachers and the specific consequences of this influence for teachers.

Fueled by the effective schools research and school reform of the late 1970s and 1980s, the interest in understanding effective principals has increased significantly. Studies conducted during the 1980s highlighted a host of factors associated with effective school leadership. These include initiative, confidence, tolerance for ambiguity, analytic abilities, resourcefulness, vision, democratic-participatory style, listening, problem centeredness, openness, time management skills, high expectations, knowledge of curriculum, and ability to allocate resources effectively (e.g., Blase, 1987; Blumberg & Greenfield, 1986; Bossert, Dwyer, Rowan, & Lee, 1982; Brady, 1985; Brookover & Lezotte, 1977; Edmonds, 1982; Hallinger & Murphy, 1987; Hannaway & Stevens, 1985; Lipham, 1981; Peterson, 1978; Russell, Mazzarella, White, & Maurer, 1985; Wolcott, 1973). However, with few exceptions published more recently (e.g., Blase & Blase, 1998; Reitzug, 1997), concrete descriptions of how effective school principals use a wide range of strategies to influence teachers and their work are notably limited.

A study completed by Russell et al. (1985) at the University of Oregon described effective principal behaviors and linked them to the characteristics of effective schools. These authors noted, for instance, that principals who provide extra academic work for outstanding students or who encourage students to take highly challenging courses contribute to the characteristics of high expectations and clear school goals. These researchers reported more than 100 such effective principal behaviors.

Bossert et al. (1982) contributed greatly to our understanding of the relationship between leadership and teacher performance by introducing a model that links school principals' actions—such as goal setting, evaluating, monitoring, and modeling—to instructional climate (i.e., staff commitment and discipline) and instructional organization (e.g., academic curriculum and pedagogy). Student achievement outcomes are viewed as an indirect result of principals' actions that affect instructional climate and classroom organization. The theoretical model discussed by Bossert et al. was more recently tested by Heck and his associates (Heck, Larsen, & Marcoulides, 1990; Heck & Marcoulides, 1993). They found several behaviors, including communicating instructional goals, working to keep faculty morale high, and establishing an orderly environment, that enhance school climate. Other leadership behaviors—developing school goals, securing resources for programs, evaluating curricular programs—were identified with promoting instructional organization. Heck and his associates demonstrated that the two classes of leader behavior (i.e., instructional climate and instructional organization) positively affected student achievement in the schools they studied. Their conclusions regarding the importance of a range of informal principal behaviors are consistent with the teachers' data we discuss in this book. They write:

> Our results indicate that many of the important instructional leadership variables influencing school achievement are not related to the regular clinical supervision of teachers. . . . While regularly observing teachers and conferencing with them regarding instructional improvement is admittedly an important aspect, our results show that principals' time and attention are focused on a variety of additional activities. Many behaviors, that are more informal and strategic, cluster into the constructs of instructional organization and school climate and impact student achievement as well. Some of these efforts involve clarifying, coordinating, and communicating a unified school educational purpose to teachers, students, and the community. Effective principals appear to build a sense of teamwork at the school. (Heck et al., 1990, pp. 120–121)

In sum, although the study of instructional aspects of leadership and student achievement has been shown to be complex and empirically challenging (Hallinger & Heck, 1996a, 1996b), and although a number of scholars have acknowledged the dearth of studies of the relationships among leadership, teaching, and student achievement (Leithwood, Begley, & Cousins, 1990), some direct and indirect links to student achievement have been found and confirmed by recent work. In fact, Leithwood, Louis, Anderson, and Wahlstrom (2004b) have determined that leadership effects on student learning are actually underestimated, with the total direct and indirect effects comprising about a quarter of total school effects (Leithwood & Jantzi, 2000). We can conclude, then, that our commitment to enhancing leadership as a prime element in successful school improvement is warranted.

For more detailed information from exemplary research on the positive correlations between school leadership and student achievement, see Waters, Marzano, and McNulty's (2003) study, *Balanced Leadership: What 30 Years of Research Tells Us About the Effect of Leadership on Student Achievement.* Waters et al. highlight 21 key leadership responsibilities related to higher achievement according to effect size; primary among these are situational awareness, intellectual stimulation, being a change agent, gathering input, developing the culture, and monitoring student learning. It is important to stress that Waters et al.'s research is consistent with that of others with respect to the basics of successful leadership and, as such, underscores the importance of a transformational approach to leadership (e.g., Hallinger & Heck's, 1999, categories of leader practices include purposes, people, and structures and social systems; Conger & Kanungo's, 1998, categories include visioning, efficacy-building, and context-changing strategies; and Leithwood's, 1996, categories include setting directions, developing people, and redesigning the organization).

TRANSFORMATIONAL LEADERSHIP

The meaning of transformational leadership evolved from Burns's (1978) conceptualization of leaders who motivate followers to accomplish goals that represent shared values and beliefs. Unlike transactional leadership which is based on an exchange, transformational leadership changes the level of follower commitment to organizational goals. Burns views leadership as a moral enterprise. Bass (1985, 1988, 1990) first operationalized Burns's constructs of transformational and transactional leadership with his Multifactor Leadership Questionnaire (MLQ). The MLQ has undergone several revisions but generally measures four dimensions of transformational leadership (charisma, inspirational motivation, intellectual stimulation, and individualized consideration) and two dimensions of transactional leadership (management by exception and contingent reward), plus nonleadership or the absence of leadership.

More relevant to the field of education has been the extensive work of Kenneth Leithwood (1994) and his colleagues (Leithwood & Jantzi, 2000; Leithwood et al., 1996b) who created surveys based on the MLQ to measure leadership in education. They also are credited with numerous studies demonstrating the relationship between the use of transformational leadership and teacher motivation, school climate, and student achievement (Leithwood et al., 1996b, 2004a, 2004b). Leithwood's conceptualization includes previous factors of both transformational and transactional leadership. Both he and Bass contend that these two types of leadership build on one another rather than compete as distinct styles. Leithwood and Jantzi (2000) identified seven dimensions of transformational school leadership: (1) building vision and establishing goals, (2) providing intellectual stimulation, (3) offering individualized support, (4) modeling best practices and organizational values, (5) demonstrating high performance expectations, (6) creating a productive school culture, and (7) developing structures for shared decision making. Considerable overlap with Bass is obvious but there is clearly no emphasis on charismatic leadership in Leithwood's work. In later chapters we discuss the role of charisma in leadership as well as how our findings about how effective principals positively influence teachers—findings produced by using grounded qualitative research protocols—are related to Leithwood and his colleagues' findings generated through survey research.

PRINCIPALS' INFLUENCE ON TEACHERS: A BRIEF HISTORICAL OVERVIEW

Studies conducted during the 1970s, 1980s, and 1990s of how school principals use power and influence in their interactions with teachers have helped to advance understanding of school-based leadership. In this group of studies, principal effectiveness has been associated with the use of positive forms of influence with teachers rather than formal authority. Isherwood (1973) found that principals who demonstrate charisma, expertise, and human relations skills heighten teachers' loyalty to the principal and improve teacher satisfaction. Studies have shown how principals have granted teachers direct participation in decision making and consistently professed confidence in teachers' abilities; the latter often include initiation of teacher leadership in schools (Allen, Glickman, & Hensley, 1998; Crow, Matthews, & McCleary, 1996; Riordan & da Costa, 1998). Furthermore, building trust has been shown to be a key leadership behavior (Short & Greer, 1997), just as principals' use of persuasion is significantly related to the degree of consensus that teachers perceive in schools (Muth, 1973). Hanson (1976) discovered that in innovative schools, public praise by administrators results in desired modifications of teacher behavior. Hanson also found that principals who describe appropriate professional conduct positively influence teachers.

Studies of principal influence have shown how important informal power is to working effectively with teachers. Treslan and Ryan (1986) learned that teachers are much more responsive to principals' influence attempts based on human relations skills and technical expertise than to the use of hierarchical authority. Administrators' attempts to define school values (Firestone & Wilson, 1985), interpersonal competencies (Blase, 1987; Blumberg & Greenfield, 1986; Bredeson, 1986), support (Brady, 1985; Hoy & Brown, 1988; Reiss & Hoy, 1998), and vision (Blumberg & Greenfield, 1986), for instance, were found to be very effective in influencing teachers. Leithwood and Jantzi (1990) and Blase and Blase (1998) found that principals who rely on such strategies as staff development, communication about values, power sharing, and the use of symbols are able to foster collaborative relationships among teachers. Johnson (1984) and Blase and Roberts (1994) indicated that expertise, personal example, distribution of resources, and expressed interest favorably affect teachers. Johnston and Venable (1986) linked participatory decision making to greater teacher loyalty to principals. High and Achilles (1986) concluded that such behaviors as enabling, norm setting, and expertise are effective means of influence with teachers in high-achieving schools. With regard to effects on teachers' commitment, involvement, and innovativeness, Sheppard (1996) learned that promoting teachers' professional development is the most influential leadership behavior at both the elementary and the high school levels. Lastly, studies of transformational leadership—a broad approach to school leadership—found a relationship between principal behaviors and the existence of an effective, collaborative, innovative school culture (Conger & Kanungo, 1994; Leithwood, Tomlinson, & Genge, 1996a; Sergiovanni, 1992).

Recent scholarly work focusing on critical aspects of principal influence on teachers has emphasized (1) developing shared understandings about the school as an organization, its activities, goals, sense of purpose, or vision (this is derived from goal-based theories of human motivation which indicate that people are motivated by compelling, challenging, and achievable goals from which a sense of identity is gained) (Bandura, 1986); (2) developing people (i.e., the need for principals to be instructional leaders who have not only knowledge of the technical work that teachers do but also the emotional intelligence (Goleman, Boyatzis, & McKee, 2002) to utilize teachers' capacities, increase their enthusiasm, reduce their frustrations, and convey a sense of mission); and (3) redesigning the school (this is derived from empirical work about the nature of professional learning communities, which emphasizes strengthening the school culture, modifying its structures, and building collaborative processes) (Leithwood et al., 2004a).

Some Concluding Remarks

During the past several decades some noteworthy gains have been made toward understanding the principal-teacher relationship, especially as it relates to influence. Most of the studies noted, however, focus on teachers' and/or principals' perceptions of the types of power that principals use. These studies correlate types of administrative power with a limited number of variables, such as teacher satisfaction or loyalty, rather than focusing on effective principals per se. One qualitative study examined the "general" perspectives of effective principals (Blumberg & Greenfield, 1986); it did not investigate how principals influence teachers. Another qualitative study focused specifically on the communication styles of principals vis-à-vis teachers (Bredeson, 1986). More directly, qualitative studies completed by Hanson (1976) and Leithwood and Jantzi (1990) explored different aspects of principal influence in relation to teachers; each generated some data regarding strategies. In contrast to the study discussed in this book (with the exception of studies by Blase & Blase in 2001 and 2004), few studies have produced detailed descriptions of the range of strategies that effective principals use to influence teachers' growth and development.

The data presented in the following chapters were taken from a larger qualitative study that investigated teachers' perceptions of the strategies used by all types of principals to influence them. This total database was subsequently divided into strategies employed by open and effective principals and those used by principals whom teachers viewed as closed and ineffective.

The data discussed throughout this book focus specifically on understanding teachers' perspectives regarding only the strategies used by open and effective principals. Consistent with open-ended research methods, no definitions of "open and effective" were presented on the questionnaire that teachers completed for the study. Doing this would have limited teachers' freedom to discuss their own views of open and effective principals. The study also explored teachers' views about why they considered the strategies used by principals to be effective, as well as the purposes (goals) they attributed to principals' use of such strategies.

In addition, our study examined the effect of school principals on the cognitive, affective, and behavioral aspects of teachers' work. To our knowledge, no research has used qualitative research methods to investigate the full range of strategies that principals typically employ in their work with teachers or the consequences of such strategies for teachers themselves. A large sample of teachers participated in the study, thus adding to the credibility of the findings. The open-ended questionnaire used to collect data was administered to over 1,200 teachers. Of these, 836 focused on the strategies used by open and effective principals. Analysis of the questionnaires produced detailed descriptions of 1,323 strategies used by effective principals. It is this portion of the total database from which this book was written. (See the Resource starting on page 130 for a full description of the research problem, sample, and procedures.)

This book discusses the strategies used by effective transformational principals and how such strategies positively influence teachers. Generally speaking, the strategies appear here in terms of the frequency with which they were reported, from most frequent to least frequent. Chapters 2 through 9 describe the effective strategies and related tactics and practices, and their effect on teachers. Guidelines for reflection drawn from the research data are presented in the closing pages of each chapter. Although each chapter focuses on only certain influence strategies, we must emphasize that effective and open principals used most of the strategies described throughout this book. In the final chapter (Chapter 10), we present conclusions from our research and challenge the reader to reflect on the applicability of the strategies of open and effective principals in restructuring the schools of tomorrow. The methods used to collect and analyze the data we used for this book are discussed in the Resource.

Note: We wish to acknowledge Jo Blase for her contributions to this revised edition and to the authorship of this chapter.

CHAPTER TWO

The Power of Praise

When I am in [the principal's] office taking care of business and he sees me, or when I peek into his office to say hello, he takes time to give me some kind of feedback. Sometimes it is as casual as, "You look peppy today." Sometimes it is to comment on something I'm involved in: "The Drill Team sure was impressive last night. How cohesive, proud, and disciplined they looked!" He'll tell me about a student's comment that I have a lot of energy and organizational skills which make my class fun. The main thing, no matter what he says, is he is sincere. It's not B.S. and isn't dished out just for the sake of it. . . . Credibility is important. I'm not sure he does this consciously . . . it's just the way he is. He has good interpersonal skills, and that probably carries him a long way and is responsible for his effectiveness.

I feel good, inspired, motivated. It reminds me that it sure is easy to make someone's day, and we need to take time to [do so] more often. Being motivated makes us do a better job. I'm sure it helps me remain positive and flexible.

—A high school teacher

Of all the strategies used to influence teachers' work, praise was the most frequently reported and was perceived as one of the most effective by teachers in our study. Interestingly, praise is usually dismissed as a professional influence strategy and only in recent years has it appeared in descriptions of effective school leadership (Blase & Blase, 2001, 2003; Blase, Blase, Anderson, & Dungan, 1997; Murphy & Louis, 1994).

Our teachers clearly valued personal compliments and individual attention from their principals. The strength of praise, an example of reward power (French & Raven, 1959), in influencing an individual or group depends on its value to that individual or group (Hoy & Miskel, 2005; Yukl, 2006). Why then the discrepancy between what teachers perceive to be such a crucial role for principals and what school effectiveness and school effects researchers discuss as key correlates of leader effectiveness?

Perhaps, as Greenfield (1987) hints, it may be taken for granted that principals routinely praise teachers. After all, teacher performance assessment instruments invariably include indicators of how teachers reinforce student behavior; positive reinforcement is universally accepted as a correlate of effective teaching. Principals, as former teachers, may be expected automatically to translate this teaching behavior to the leadership domain. That some principals are effective in doing so is revealed in our data. Nevertheless, with few exceptions (e.g., Blase & Blase, 2001, 2004) praise remains conspicuously underreported in the literature about effective school leadership. For this reason, it may be underused by school principals.

Perhaps principals are familiar with the power of praise, but in their haste to attend to numerous other aspects of the job, the importance of praising teachers may be displaced (Boris-Schater & Langer, 2006). Terrence Deal (1987) was among the first to recognize that much of the scholarly literature (with regard to the principal's role) ignores important aspects of schools. He argues that schools should be examined through multiple lenses. Principals must attend to other critical organizational dimensions in addition to instruction. They must be instructional leaders as well as counselors or parents, engineers or supervisors, contenders or referees, and heroes or poets. As counselors/parents, principals add to personal growth and development with praise, advice, and affection. The nurturing function, according to Deal and other scholars (e.g., Beck & Murphy, 1994; Deal & Peterson, 1990; Evers, 1992) is one of the most time-consuming demands of the principalship. Unfortunately, principals who are eager to develop their "instructional leadership" skills or deal with other aspects of the job may do so at the expense of building viable professional relationships with teachers.

Viewing principals as counselors or parents, as Deal (1987) suggests, may appear a bit paternalistic to many teachers, thereby reducing teachers' stature. Even if Deal's analogy is scorned, his counsel nonetheless may be valid. We reiterate that in our data, praise is the most frequently mentioned influence strategy used by effective, transformational principals. Its role in leader effectiveness should not be ignored or taken for granted.

WHY PRAISE?

Given that principals are expected to assume many roles in schools and that the roles of transformational leader and instructional leader alone are multifaceted, why do effective transformational principals devote so much time to praising teachers? Although one intent in conducting this study was to identify effective strategies used by principals to influence *teacher* performance, it may be true that praise also satisfies personal needs of the principals themselves. From several studies of successful school principals, Blase and Blase (1996, 2001, 2004) learned that such principals have high needs for expressing and receiving affection and warmth. Principals who are successful may be sensitive to the interpersonal needs of teachers because they themselves derive satisfaction similarly.

In addition to the personal satisfaction they may derive from praising teachers, according to our data, effective principals also use praise as a strategy for influencing teachers' attitudes and behavior. Teachers in our study linked the use of praise specifically to principals' goals of promoting and reinforcing classroom performance. This is consistent with effective transformational leadership (Blase & Blase, 2001; Leithwood, 1994; Leithwood & Jantzi, 2000; Leithwood, Tomlinson, & Genge, 1996a) and the effects research (Marzano, 2000; Waters, Marzano, & McNulty, 2003). As an influence strategy, praise is used most often with individual teachers; effective principals commend teachers for their instructional and classroom management efforts. Recognition of individual teachers' strengths is viewed as a means of maintaining and developing teachers' skills while promoting teachers' confidence and satisfaction.

Whereas other influence strategies may be used to encourage teachers' involvement in aspects of schooling that transcend the classroom, goals associated with the use of praise are related directly to enhancing instructional performance and therefore stand an excellent chance of affecting both teaching and student learning (Blase & Blase, 2001, 2004; Leithwood, 1994). Praise also is used to build school culture and climate, including faculty cohesiveness and support for school goals. Schein (1985) argues that building an effective culture is the most important aspect of leadership; an effective organizational culture influences the way teachers respond to events, unites teachers and administrators, and gives purpose and meaning to work (Deal & Peterson, 1990).

TEACHER REACTIONS TO THE USE OF PRAISE

We have all heard the occasional grumblings of administrators uncomfortable with overt displays of affection or encouragement (they claim not to be the "touchy-feely" type), or the administrator who says, "I hire good teachers and leave them alone." Similarly, we have heard the teacher who disdains such expressions of approval, viewing them as condescending or patronizing. Is the use of praise necessary and effective for improving teaching performance? To answer this question, we again turn to the responses of our teachers.

The teachers in our study viewed praise as a positive and effective influence strategy. Praise from their principals helped boost their esteem, confidence, and pride. Many reported that positive reinforcement left them feeling "encouraged," "appreciated," and "recognized":

The principal often writes personal notes to individual faculty members, encouraging, complimenting, and just giving "strokes." These are found in our mailboxes at school or sometimes sent out to our homes. She also sends out notes to the entire faculty complimenting them for a job well done. She makes me feel that what I do is appreciated, and these actions

*give me positive thoughts about the principal . . . I know how
busy her schedule is. When I feel that what I do is noticed and
appreciated, I have a better feeling about my job and try to do a
better job.*

—A middle school teacher

Maslow (1970) describes five levels of needs in humans:
(1) basic physiological needs, (2) security and safety, (3) social affil-
iation and growth, (4) self-esteem and recognition, and (5) self-
actualization. He argues that if lower order needs are unmet, people
tend not to respond to higher order needs. From a review of relevant
studies of teachers, Owens and Valesky (2007) concluded that
esteem is teachers' greatest need and for teachers to achieve higher
levels of motivation, they must "achieve feelings of professional
self-worth, competence, and respect; to be seen as people of achievement, professionals who are influential in their workplaces, growing
persons with opportunities ahead to develop even greater competence and a sense of accomplishment" (p. 388). The implications are
clear: All principals need to do much more with regard to praising
teachers, especially for their work on behalf of students.

In addition to promoting greater esteem and satisfaction, the use
of praise increases teachers' sense of belonging. Because their principals take the time to recognize their contributions, teachers feel
that they are "important members of the team." Others said they feel
"loved" and "respected" by their principals.

As a strategy for influencing teacher behavior, the use of praise is
particularly successful. Teachers reported that the positive feelings
associated with praise led to increased motivation. Increases in teacher
motivation appear to have a direct effect on classroom practices and
may also affect student learning (Leithwood & Jantzi, 2000). Teachers
feel "inspired" and "enthusiastic." Their loyalty and dedication grow.
Because of her principal's appreciation, one teacher declared, "I
wouldn't think of not doing a good job. I would feel guilty." Another
concurred: "I try to do my best to live up to his comments."

Praise affects teacher behavior along several dimensions.
Generally, teachers attempt to comply with the expectations principals

implied in the use of praise. According to teachers, performance compliance concerns instruction and use of time:

- "I try harder to be creative in my teaching."
- "Indeed, more time is spent planning."
- "I work harder. This means I don't just put in eight hours a day. I work until I'm finished."

Recognizing how praise positively affects them, teachers often model the practice by using a more positive discipline approach, including frequent praise, with students. Modeling is used both in the classroom and throughout the school building:

- "I'm more positive . . . open and patient with students."
- "I look for something to praise the kids about."
- "I find myself trying to emulate [the principal's] positiveness not only with my students but with parents and other teachers."

Finally, teachers reported that praise affected their support for principals. Some teachers acknowledged reciprocating:

- "I praise him in return."
- "I'm quicker to support the principal."

Others volunteered their time and energy to help principals:

- "I'll do 'extras' for her."
- "I'm more apt to volunteer for projects she needs help on."

It appears then that praise is an effective strategy for improving school climate and building school culture because it enhances teacher morale and teachers' attitudes toward students. It also enhances the amount of effort they put forth on many classroom matters, especially to improve teaching and learning.

ON POTENCY AND UBIQUITY

Our research has produced indisputable evidence of the power of praise as an influence strategy with teachers. We have suggested that some educators—teachers and principals—may feel uncomfortable with this strategy. Still, we cannot deny its potency. We have gathered substantial evidence of the positive effects of praise on both attitudes and behaviors of teachers. Two questions surface with regard to this finding. First, how do we account for the singular effect of a strategy that may be viewed as "obvious" or "common sense"? And if the potency of the strategy is obvious, why is it not used by more school principals?

Educators invariably agree that their work is plagued by difficulties. Means and ends are only loosely connected; seldom are we certain that what we actually do in the classroom positively affects students' lives. In one of the most respected studies of the sociology of teaching, Dan Lortie (1975) observed that teaching is filled with "endemic uncertainties" related to difficulties of assessing individual student outcomes and the quality of teaching, as well as of multiple role expectations (pp. 134–61). Because the link between what teachers do and its effect on students is uncertain, teachers must rely on self-evaluations of performance. Yet most individuals have needs for recognition and approval that remain unfulfilled by self-evaluation alone. Other studies confirm the existence of similar problems for teachers (Blase & Blase, 2001, 2004; Lieberman & Miller, 1984; Rosenholtz & Simpson, 1990).

Uncertainties and self-doubts could be mollified by approval from others. Unfortunately, formal performance evaluations, no matter how outstanding, offer teachers little consolation. A positive evaluation indicates minimal competence; seldom is it used for purposes of recognition or advancement. And, as Lortie (1975) notes, veteran teachers work day after day knowing that they can be replaced by novices!

Because teaching also is characterized by the isolation of the classroom, there are few opportunities for interaction with other adults. Teachers rarely observe or are observed by other teachers. They spend nearly every working minute communicating with children—often as many as 150 children per day. It is not surprising that they respond so appreciatively and enthusiastically to adult interaction and feedback. Unless cooperative experiences such as peer coaching become commonplace, administrators are the only external adult referents by which teachers judge their work.

Perhaps the most revealing observation from our study is that teachers reported being influenced by praise only when it was related to their professional performance. Although they may have been complimented for appearances (e.g., a new suit or hairstyle) or praised for accomplishments outside the school, only classroom-related praise was reported as a source of considerable influence. To be effective with teachers, it seems, praise must be connected to professional accomplishments. Waters, Marzano, and McNulty (2003) reported that school leaders who reinforce teachers' focus on instructional improvement may affect student achievement

Earlier, we asked the question, "Why praise teachers?" The more obvious question now seems to be, "Why not?" Unfortunately, the same barriers that inhibit teacher interaction also limit teacher-administrator communication. With many teachers to observe, each in a different enclosed location, even informal assessments of teacher performance are time-consuming. But to reinforce positive teacher behaviors, observation is mandatory. (What would we praise them for if we did not find out how well they were doing?) Thus, even for principals who value informal classroom visits and are comfortable expressing compliments and gratitude, the demands on their time are exacerbated by the structural isolation of teaching. Nevertheless, despite the difficulties in observing and acknowledging classroom performance, some principals are particularly adept at recognizing teacher contributions to school success.

Opportunities and Methods

How and when do effective transformational principals praise teachers' professional performance? The answer, according to our teachers: Principals capitalize on every available opportunity to compliment teachers; their praise consists of brief but sincere remarks and gestures.

Although time and structure may limit the number of opportunities to praise individual teachers, effective principals take advantage of other situations. Many teachers reported that their principals regularly use group praise. Principals are able to reach many teachers at once by complimenting them at faculty meetings, in conferences with smaller groups of teachers, over the intercom, or by e-mail. As evidenced by the remarks of several teachers, principals use such occasions to express praise without qualification:

- "He expresses a complete faith and belief in his faculty . . . says we are the chosen ones . . . the best faculty in the state."
- "He starts and ends every meeting by complimenting the faculty for their hard work."
- "Every Friday she tells us how hard we worked."

We learned from our study that praise can be an effective influence strategy even when it is not communicated directly to teachers. Teachers reported knowing how their principals feel about their work from comments the principals made to others. Although perhaps not intended as a means of influence, teachers did learn of these remarks to others and were impressed by them. As one teacher boasted, "He brags on us every chance he gets."

Group praise is not, we found, used by effective principals to compensate for a lack of individual praise. Quite the contrary, principals intersperse frequent and specific individual praise with group praise. They mention individuals by name at faculty meetings and in conversations with others. Informal verbal compliments are commonplace; one teacher called them "one-minute praises." Another noted the deliberate effort of his principal to praise teachers: "She catches me doing something right and says so." Although principals most often comment on some aspect of teacher performance that they have witnessed, compliments from students or parents also are relayed to teachers.

In addition to oral praise, the principals described in our study wrote brief notes to individual teachers. After observing classes, many principals left short notes of praise on teachers' desks. Others placed complimentary notes in the mailboxes of individual teachers.

Finally, principals often express praise nonverbally. Especially effective during the classroom observation where the principal hopes to be unobtrusive, the nonverbal gesture communicates immediate approval. This technique takes several forms, all appreciated by our teachers:

- "She touches me on the shoulder to show her appreciation."
- "Simple smiles tell me a lot."

Thus, transformational principals rely on brief, usually informal, verbal and nonverbal praise to influence individual teachers and teacher groups. It should be noted that variety and frequency of praise appear to be as important as the particular techniques used (e.g., written memos, e-mails, comments to others, public address announcements, pats on the back). It is important to stress that teachers in our study often spoke of praise not as an influence strategy used by a principal, but as a part of the principal's character. Praise is sincere, genuine, and even natural for these principals. Needless to say, praise is not given to teachers in an impersonal and mechanical way, but rather in a heartfelt symbolic manner to acknowledge important accomplishments and express personal appreciation (Yukl, 2006). Moreover, such recognition of teachers was related to teachers' perceptions of their own empowerment: concern for teachers' work and support of that work are key characteristics related to teachers' belief in their own empowerment (Rinehart, Short, Short, & Eckley, 1998).

TIPS FROM TEACHERS

Our data indicate that in spite of the endemic uncertainties and structural isolation of teaching, effective principals find many opportunities to commend teachers and that, to be effective, praise need not be formal or lengthy. The particular behaviors for which the teachers in our study were praised also are revealing. In every case reported, teachers indicated that the praise that influenced them most was evoked by their work. Thus, on the basis of our teachers' reports, we offer the following suggestions to consider in the context of your own school setting.

1. Praise sincerely.

   Teachers view praise from effective principals as genuine. Rather than perceiving it only as an influence strategy, teachers see its expression as comfortable and natural for their principals. Praise does not appear contrived or awkward; it is congruent with other behaviors and personal characteristics of principals (See Blase & Blase [2004] for a description of the adverse effects of inauthentic and inappropriate praise given to teachers by some school principals).

2. Maximize the use of nonverbal communication.

   Effective principals use nonverbal gestures such as smiles, nods, and touches to communicate approval. Although not used as an exclusive form of praise, this technique is commonly employed during informal walk-throughs and formal classroom observations to avoid the disruption of verbal praise.

3. Schedule time for teacher recognition.

   Many teachers report that their principals praise them on a regular basis. Some principals choose the beginning or the end of faculty meetings. Recognition of faculty at student assemblies also is common. Others choose to announce faculty accomplishments over the public address system at the end of each week. Many principals routinely praise teachers during their tours of schools. It is clear that effective principals build time for praise into their busy schedules. Although the use of praise seems "natural," the neophyte might become more adept at the use of this strategy by consciously scheduling opportunities for recognition. As the practice becomes automatic and comfortable, additional forums for praise might be added.

4. Write brief personal notes or e-mails to compliment individuals.

To praise individual teachers, transformational principals often rely on written messages. These brief notes are frequently handwritten and personalized. In a recent study of successful transformational principals, Blase and Phillips (2008) found that personalized e-mails also were used to compliment teachers. Our teachers did not report being influenced by written acknowledgment of group efforts.

5. Show pride in teachers by boasting!

Teachers often learn of their principals' judgments of their work from others. Principals express pride in their teachers to parents, colleagues, and others in the community.

6. Praise briefly.

To be effective, praise need not be formal or lengthy. Teachers appreciate many forms of recognition that last only seconds. Thus, short accolades delivered in a variety of forums using both verbal and nonverbal techniques can be effective without placing excessive demands on the principal's time.

7. Target praise to teachers' work.

Because of the isolation and uncertainty characteristic of the profession, teachers are most responsive to praise bestowed for school-related success. Whenever possible, principals should commend specific professional accomplishments of individual teachers, particularly classroom practices that have a direct effect on student learning. Group praise can be used to increase the opportunities for recognition, but it too should be tied to specific achievements.

CHAPTER THREE

Influencing by Expecting

The main tactic used by my principal in trying to influence us is emphasizing that what we do is "for our babies." For example, the county did not have a breakfast program, and our principal thought we should. This is a very economically depressed area, and she saw a need to enhance the nutritional well-being of our children. There was resistance to this from the educational community, but her general emphasis on "our babies" being taken care of in every way was the power of her argument which proved successful.

[As a result,] I find all my thoughts are on the children and what I can do to totally enhance their school experience. We all concentrate our efforts on the children. Because [the principal] is sincere in her commitment to children, I feel proud and privileged to be associated with her and her ideas.

—An elementary school teacher

High expectations for student academic achievement is prominent on any list of effective schools characteristics (e.g., Edmonds, 1979; Purkey & Smith, 1983). The expectations of students, parents, teachers, and administrators are all positively related to student outcomes (Brookover, Beady, Flood, Schweitzer, & Wisenbaker, 1979; Glenn & McLean, 1981; Rutter, Maugham, Mortimore, Ouston, & Smith, 1979; Teddlie, Falkowski, Stringfield, Desselle, & Garvue, 1984; Weil et al., 1984). Not surprisingly, there is often a consistency about expectations among these multiple groups: When parents, teachers, and principals hold high expectations for students, students are likely to expect more of themselves (Heck, Larsen, & Marcoulides, 1990; Heck & Marcoulides, 1993; Marzano, 1998; Marzano, Gaddy, & Dean, 2000; Marzano, Pickering, & Pollock, 2001; Sheppard, 1996).

More specifically, the influence of principals' expectations on student achievement has been investigated by educational productivity and school effects researchers. The expectations that principals hold for both student performance and teacher performance are positively related to student academic success (Leithwood & Jantzi, 2000; Marzano, Waters, & McNulty, 2005; National Association of Elementary School Principals [NAESP], 2001); even so, causal statements regarding the role of principal expectations in influencing student achievement cannot be made. Logic tells us that this relationship is probably an indirect one: Few principals have time to interact directly with students on a daily basis. Teachers provide the obvious link. Communication with teachers about expectations for students has been heralded as a critical component of school climate that affects student outcomes (Blase & Blase, 2004; Heck et al., 1990; Leithwood & Jantzi, 2000; Marzano et al., 2005; Murphy & Datnow, 2003).

At first glance, we may conclude that principals' expectations have a power somewhat like the ominous warnings in chain letters. Teachers feel convinced or compelled to pass the principal's "message" along to their students. The principal's expectations mushroom as teachers spread the word to their awaiting charges.

We know that expectations regarding ability, aptitude, values, and pedagogy are not accepted unquestioningly, however. Teachers do not passively adopt their principal's values and beliefs and translate these into compatible teaching behaviors that, in turn, affect student performance. The chain letter metaphor breaks down because any understanding of the principal's influence must take into account individual teacher differences in values and understandings. Principals' expectations for changes in teacher attitudes and behavior gain meaning and derive influence only as they are interpreted and evaluated by teachers.

EXPECTATIONS FOR WHAT?

Our data indicate that effective transformational principals use expectations to achieve two broad goals: changes in attitudes and changes in behaviors. Principals are aware of their own limitations in influencing teacher attitudes; they assume that changes in attitudes often follow changes in teacher behavior. A teacher reported that her principal, for example, believes very strongly in the benefits of reserving time blocks for reading. How can the principal use expectations to influence teachers to use this new method? As we see it, she has two options: She can expect teachers to see the importance of the method (a change in attitude), or she can expect teachers to try the method (a change in behavior).

Our findings suggest that principals attack from both fronts. They recognize that some teachers are influenced by expectations because they perceive the principal as having expert knowledge in an area; indeed, principals' expectations are often driven by research-based practices that enhance student progress across content areas (Cawelti, 2004). For other teachers, however, seeing is believing; changes in their attitudes result from their own evaluation of a new method as it is implemented. We learned that effective transformational principals communicate the expectation that their teachers "give things a chance" before passing judgment.

Consider two statements to teachers regarding a silent reading program:

- "I expect student test scores in reading to increase if students are given uninterrupted reading time each morning."
- "I expect you and your students to read silently for 15 minutes each morning."

The first statement, it seems, is intended to convince teachers of the value of silent reading; behavioral changes are only implied. The second is intended to change teachers' behavior (time allocation) regardless of their attitudes. It appears that effective principals recognize the separate and collective effect of both kinds of statements;

thus, they frequently use expectancy statements aimed at changing both attitudes and behaviors.

What are the specific goals of transformational principals who want to change the attitudes and behaviors of teachers? Although expectations occasionally reflect school district policies and programs, our data indicate that the expectations of effective principals are largely derived from their personal values regarding appropriate human interaction and school purposes. These principals are not mere messengers of expectations for district directives; they communicate their own personal visions of ideal school climate and processes related to respect for students, teacher classroom behavior, teacher-parent communication, curriculum, and pedagogy. As we discuss in later chapters, however, transformational principals involve teachers in setting school goals. Thus, the expectations they convey are shared by others in the school community. Consequently, the entire school community (not just the principal) is responsible for leadership through expectation (Ackerman, Donaldson, & van der Bogert, 1996; Blase & Blase, 2001, 2004, 2006; Glickman, 1993).

Respect for Students

Respect for students is a prominent theme evident in the language and behavior of effective principals. Teachers are expected to demonstrate respect and encourage student self-esteem. Principals associate these behaviors with both improved student discipline and achievement.

Teachers report that they are expected to use directed praise; that is, students' individual strengths are to be highlighted to project respect (Marzano, 2000; Walberg & Haertel, 1997). Nonspecific praise (e.g., "Erin, you're doing so much better") should be replaced with clarification of both expectations and perceived outcomes ("Ramón, I'm so pleased that you're remembering to cross out the identities to simplify your fractions").

Recognizing and accepting individual differences is another important aspect of respect for students (Capper, Frattura, & Keyes, 2000; Gregory & Chapman, 2005; Joyce, Weil, & Calhoun, 2000; Stone, 2004). Teachers stated that transformational principals encourage them to "find something good" in each student. Very often, recognition programs are developed in academic and nonacademic realms. For instance, one principal videotapes classrooms to enhance student self-esteem—all the students present thus are able to admire themselves at work. Other principals recognize students for good citizenship. Many create possibilities for a variety of students to achieve such rewards. Respect for students of all abilities is often an explicit goal of transformational principals described by our teachers. Teachers are expected to treat all students with dignity. Asking two typically "detached" students to remove trash from the play area during recess and later publicly recognizing their accomplishment is one such tactic.

Effective principals work to enhance teachers' sense of efficacy in dealing with students of all abilities and cultural backgrounds. No student is presumed incapable of learning or improving. Teaching efficacy goes beyond a belief in one's own competence in terms of knowledge and skills (Dembo & Gibson, 1985; Tschannen-Moran, Hoy, & Hoy, 1998). In a study of school climate and efficacy, Lasserre (1989) found that teachers reported higher levels of teaching efficacy in schools where there were greater incentives for professionalism and an emphasis on hard work and dedication. Echoing the findings of earlier efficacy studies (e.g., Armor et al., 1976), Lasserre concluded that a successful education program reflects a belief that all students can learn and that principals' expectations can influence that belief.

Teacher efficacy contributes to greater effort and persistence, according to Tschannen-Moran, Hoy, and Hoy (1998). Increases in teacher efficacy have been associated with principals' willingness to provide resources and buffer teachers from disruptive factors (Lee, Dedick, & Smith, 1991), model appropriate behavior and provide rewards for performance (Hipp & Bredeson, 1995), improve school climate (Hoy & Woolfolk, 1993), and initiate and support meaningful staff development (Blase & Blase, 2004, 2006).

Influencing Teacher Behavior

Another purpose associated with the use of expectations is the modification of teacher behavior. In some cases, efforts to modify teacher behavior are related to expectations that teachers convey respect for students. For example, teachers describe effective principals as expecting them to "control their tempers." They are expected to model the kind of behavior expected of students and to demonstrate a "dignified," "positive approach" to student discipline.

Transformational principals also use expectations to influence other aspects of school climate, including faculty relations. They often speak of the cohesiveness of their faculties, the idea of "family," and of "being in this together." Kouzes and Posner (1990) refer to this as a way of "enlisting others." These authors further note the effect of language in "giving life" to an expectation. Less effective principals say, "I believe all students can learn." Unconvinced principals even deny that the belief is theirs: "Research says that. . . ." The language of the effective principal, however, denotes conviction as well as an expectation: "We know that all students can learn." Of course, effective principals will deny neither their own values nor empirical evidence, but they do use language ("we") to encourage unity.

Teacher-Parent Communication

The use of expectations to influence teacher behavior is not limited to school climate factors. Principals use expectations to enhance school-home communication as well. The goal is conveyed both overtly and suggestively. Teachers report that effective principals encourage contact with parents. Research demonstrates that parental involvement in education (e.g., involvement in instruction at home, involvement in school governance) affect student achievement, attendance, homework completion, and motivation (Epstein, 2001; Henderson & Mapp, 2002; Sheldon, 2003; Walberg & Haertel, 1997).

Curriculum and Pedagogy

Expectations are effectively used to communicate goals for programs, curriculum, and teaching methods. Earlier we mentioned a principal who emphasized the value of reading by implementing a silent reading program. Changes in scheduling were used to reinforce the verbal message that all teachers were expected to support this program.

Preference for particular teaching methods often is revealed in the expectations of the effective principals that teachers described. Through their words and actions, teachers know whether their principals favor, for instance, direct instruction, exploratory learning, or peer coaching. One teacher described the principal as having a definition of education that he explicitly differentiated from training to influence teachers to use more creative instructional methods:

> *He believes that schools must teach students how to make a living and how to live productive, meaningful lives. He constantly stresses the importance of using our classrooms to do more than train students. They must provide students with opportunities to learn to discriminate between valid and invalid information. He has made me aware that every student needs both [training and education], and only if we make this distinction will we have a balance in our educational system.*

With a renewed emphasis on mastery of basic skills, there are more and more classrooms where urban poor children engage in what can best be described as "choral yelling." Under the enthusiastic direction of their overzealous teachers, they recite (or lip-sync!) multiplication facts, language rules, or dates in history. Memorization is equated with mastery. Not so in the school of our "education" principal. It is highly unlikely that a single teacher in this school will be found "directing the chorus."

TEACHER EFFECTS

How do teachers feel when their principals expect them to think and act in particular ways? And, more important, do the expectations of principals result in any real changes in the way teachers subsequently think and act?

Our teachers told us that the subtle (and not-so-subtle) messages communicated by transformational principals are generally clear, consistent, direct, and tactful. As such, teachers tend to view the strategy very positively; they are pleased because they hear the strength of conviction and see an ability and willingness on the principal's part to model appropriate behavior. Blase and Blase (2004) found that principals who are effective instructional leaders treat teachers with respect, act on their own values and beliefs rather than in compliance with bureaucratic roles, and hold themselves accountable for their school's success. Because successful principals are willing to practice what they preach, they engender higher levels of faculty satisfaction, motivation, and efficacy. Teachers in our study also reported great responsiveness to principals who communicate and model clear and consistent expectations.

Teacher behavior and attitudes indeed are affected by principal expectations. Our findings disclose that principals' expectations enhance teachers' sensitivity to and respect for students in matters of discipline. Teachers report practicing greater self-control, consistency, and fairness in such matters. They also take on extra duties in response to their principals' expectations. One teacher started a weekly newsletter because of the principal's emphasis on school-home relations. Another spent personal time helping with a food drive (initiated by the principal) for victims of a hurricane.

Teachers reported that they usually conform to principals' expectations; they had both rational and pragmatic reasons for doing so. In the first case, they appreciate knowing what's expected, what's important, and what's valued. In the second case, they associate the use of expectations with positive outcomes such as being able to "see students and faculty growing."

Some of the teachers included in our study seem to rationalize that the benefits of complying with their principal's expectations outweigh the disadvantages. They recognize the positive outcomes of using expectations to influence other teachers, and sometimes explain that "it's not because of me" that the approach is necessary. Similar to many teachers' attitudes toward evaluation, their belief is that other teachers need more guidance and monitoring. In explaining how she felt about the principal's use of expectations to influence her behavior, one teacher stated, "I feel stressed and overwhelmed, yet I am glad that those teachers who were not performing are now forced to put up or shut up."

The negative feelings we found with regard to the use of expectations are not surprising. New expectations tax the psychological and physical strengths of teachers. When attitudes change, they must be assimilated into the existing values structure; when behaviors change, they usually displace previous behaviors.

A few of our teachers were cynical about complying with principals' expectations. They saw themselves as "playing the game" and going along with what the principal wanted without becoming personally involved or committed. Nevertheless, our research suggests that the rumblings of the occasional cynic are invalidated by the teachers who report new insights or a more reflective stance because their principals dare to challenge the status quo.

"YES, BUT. . . ."

Through our work with teachers we have been convinced that principals do have direct influence on teacher attitudes and behaviors. Teachers attest to this influence, and when working with effective principals, teachers are generally pleased with the changes in school climate and organizational processes that ensue. Teachers themselves have reported improvements in their interactions with students, their use of time, their teaching methods, their communication with parents, and their sense of belonging.

Our research provides strong evidence linking principals' use of expectations to improved teacher behavior. Equally important is the ability of this conclusion to inform practice. We are sure that the reader is now likely to be thinking, "Yes, but. . . ." "But how can I use this to change our (we hope you didn't say my) school?" "But who will be convinced just because I say I 'expect' something?" "But exactly how do these effective principals do it?" Those, in fact, are the questions that must be answered if we hope to improve practice.

We must identify the specific tactics (i.e., behaviors, practices) used by effective principals to convey what they intend to convey and achieve.

The Language of Expectations

The most obvious strategy for communicating expectations is the use of words. Our data indicate that effective principals choose a variety of words to indicate their desires. In addition to, and often preferable to, "I expect. . . ." are "Let me clarify. . . ." "I want to emphasize. . . ." "I encourage you to. . . ." and "I'd like to explain. . . ."

Our teachers reported that expectations are reinforced through repetition, clarification, and consistency. It is not enough to assert at an afternoon faculty meeting that problem-solving skills are to be incorporated into every subject area. Bombarded with new information on a variety of topics after a long day in the classroom, teachers are selective in what they choose to attend to and what they choose to ignore. When a new idea or philosophy is presented, some teachers (and principals) tell us that they usually assume that "this too shall pass." The "problem-solving approach" is filed away in that part of the brain that stores fuzzy musings on nongraded classes and democratic learning. Only when the notion is mentioned again and then again is it retrieved for further processing. In a world characterized by information overload, repetition is the key to influencing action. It is not that teachers are defiant; they simply have been conditioned to attend selectively to new information.

Whereas repetition reveals the degree of importance that principals attach to their messages, clarification seems to improve the likelihood that teachers will be able to act. The principal who expects teachers to implement a problem-solving approach clarifies what he or she means by problem solving and what he or she expects in terms of implementation. Is this to be the only approach used? Does it require a new curriculum or new materials? Are all teachers expected to use the method? Repetition then is enhanced by rephrasing and informing.

Finally, language is evaluated for its consistency. The principal who sends mixed messages with regard to his or her expectations dilutes the probability of successfully influencing listeners. Marzano et al. (2005) found that effective principals communicate clear goals for student performance and reinforce this with clear expectations for students' use of time. Our teachers reported that they are expected to use the full period of time reserved for instruction. Less effective principals are less consistent. They speak of the importance of learning in vague terms, yet they communicate conflicting expectations and accept low performance standards. In extreme cases, they even allow students to schedule physical education for three of seven periods a day, hardly a compelling argument for the importance of academic learning time!

Where Expectations Are Communicated

According to our findings, effective transformational principals take advantage of a variety of forums to project their expectations for teachers. Formal conferences with individuals and small groups, as well as general faculty meetings, are viewed as opportunities to reinforce goals. Pride in the school and its mission are common themes conveyed at student assemblies.

Formal gatherings are not the preferred situations for communicating expectations, however. More often, effective principals "drop in" during faculty committee meetings, planning periods, or between classes. Teachers often report that principals remind them of their purpose or preferred strategies during informal chats in the hallways. Informal meetings, particularly with individuals, are viewed as very effective opportunities for repeating and clarifying goals, as evidenced by the comments of this elementary school teacher:

> *The principal frequently verbally reaffirms our school's goal to provide quality education for the underprivileged in our low-SES school. He is everywhere—in classrooms, cafeteria, playground—to insure that our students have every opportunity to benefit from their education. His constant emphasis focuses us all. Every staff member can tell the goal we have for the year. I know what's important and valued in our school. I plan accordingly.*

Written communication is seen as another effective vehicle for stating expectations. Because newsletters inform in a public arena, they are used to relate selected goals and procedures. Private memos and e-mails are chosen to inform individuals or groups of areas needing improvement (Blase & Phillips, 2008).

The Power of Example

Can language alone influence teacher behavior? Imagine for a moment that you are the curator of a small art museum. You are in the process of selecting artists for an upcoming exhibit featuring the environment. Space is limited. I, as a freelance photographer, would like to persuade you to include my work in the exhibit. I tell you that black-and-white is my preferred medium, that I shoot only environmental subjects, and that I like to contrast the beauty of nature with the destructiveness of humankind. I ask you to "see" my work, but I cannot provide a portfolio. With words as my only form of persuasion, I have asked you to commit your resources and your reputation. If you are courteous, you will invite me to compete when I am more established. To yourself, you will scoff at my vanity!

Now let us suppose that a day later I return, portfolio in hand. You open the cover to reveal a single photograph. Your eyes are captivated by the graceful swan floating majestically on a crystal lake. I have used a technique known as "dodging" to lighten the swan's image, thus drawing your attention to this area. But after a moment, your eyes move to a darker image in the lower left corner. Almost hidden in the shadows, a second swan curiously pokes its beak into one of the six rings of a plastic soda pop holder. The contrast effectively invokes in you feelings of disgust and anger. Moved, you turn the page. There are no more photographs. I revert to verbal descriptions of forthcoming images. Based on a sample of one, are you now likely to "see" a place for me in your exhibition? How many more images must I produce to convince you?

Imagine now the vulnerable position of the new school principal. Expectations are clear; he or she repeats them over and over; he or she clarifies goals; messages are consistent. But what he or she wouldn't give for just one vivid photograph!

Our study reveals that teachers want and need examples of the behaviors they are expected to exhibit. Principals must rely, to a large extent, on the power of verbal persuasion, but effective principals provide examples to augment their verbal messages. The most powerful example is the principal herself or himself.

Effective principals consistently model appropriate behavior. They place themselves on exhibit as a portfolio of one, an image for others to emulate. Because they expect teachers to provide a positive environment for learning, their attitudes are positive. Because they expect teachers to maximize learning time, they minimize disruptions by limiting visitors and announcements. Because they expect teachers to engage in professional development, they read and disseminate current educational research literature.

In addition to modeling, transformational principals cite examples of specific behaviors that are consistent with their expectations. They not only expect teachers to use positive disciplinary methods, they also identify strategies from effective programs. One teacher explained how her principal tactfully persuaded her to send newsletters to parents:

My principal uses ideas of what my peers are doing to influence me in the direction she wants me to go. For example, she likes for kindergarten teachers to send home newsletters. To get me started, she showed me examples of another teacher's letters. I started sending home newsletters immediately based on this incident. This strategy was a backdoor, low intervention way of getting me to do what she valued.

Rather than dictate specific behaviors, the principal communicated expectations and showed examples. Thus, although clearly influenced by the principal, the teacher was able to own the solution:

The principal wanted to have good home-school relationships. She used a strategy that allowed me to make the decision. She didn't make me send home newsletters. I chose to do this.

GUIDELINES FOR EFFECTIVE USE OF EXPECTATIONS

In conclusion, we have learned several lessons from our investigation of how transformational principals use expectations to influence teachers. The following seven guidelines may assist the reader in developing appropriate strategies for communicating expectations that positively influence teacher behaviors and attitudes.

1. Expect.

    First and foremost, transformational principals do expect certain behaviors and attitudes of teachers. They see the result—the whole exhibition—long before it is complete, and they expect teachers to complement the theme.

2. Communicate what is expected.

    Effective principals use every available means—verbal and nonverbal—to communicate what is expected. They do not take for granted that all teachers share the same goals.

3. Communicate consistently.

    Effective principals do not send mixed messages. A common theme is evident in their words and actions.

4. Repeat, restate, clarify.

    Effective principals do not assume that a single utterance will be heeded by all. They understand the limitations to their own formal authority; they know the advantage of clarity, consistency, and redundancy in influencing teachers.

5. Seize and create opportunities.

    Effective principals use all available forums for stating and clarifying their expectations. They take advantage of faculty meetings, student assemblies, newsletters, memos, e-mails, and chance encounters.

6. Generalize expectations; personalize feedback.

Because effective principals are careful to communicate expectations consistently, their message is generally the same to all teachers (e.g., respect individual differences, discipline students positively). But because teachers react differently, the feedback they receive is personalized. Whether praising and rewarding or pointing out areas in need of improvement, principals should tailor feedback to the individual teacher. Thus, expectations may be expressed in a general faculty meeting, but suggestions for improvement are communicated privately, and rewards are tied to specific performance.

7. Provide appropriate models.

By modeling effective attitudes and practices, effective principals are their own best examples of desirable behavior. Most insist that their administrative team do so as well (Blase & Phillips, 2008). In addition, they provide specific examples of methods and programs congruent with their expectations. In sum, they become the first photograph in the exhibition, but they continuously describe the complete show while adding and inviting others to add pictures to support the theme.

CHAPTER FOUR

Influencing by Involving

Our principal is overt, informal, and extremely positive. He uses democratic procedures to make most decisions concerning our school. We have weekly leadership meetings for grade-level chairpersons so direct input comes from the teams. When something must be done in a particular manner, he very gently yet firmly requests our cooperation. Faculty meetings also are conducted in the same manner of openness and discussion, and group decisions are made. His entire manner and personality give his faculty the feeling of cooperation, togetherness, and mutual respect.

His goal is to provide an excellent education for our students in an atmosphere that is conducive to teachers' [positive] feelings and comfort. I feel that his approach to education is good and I want to copy it. I try to mirror his cooperative, friendly, positive attitude when dealing with students and parents. I feel that his approach is the best . . . and I know for a fact that he's the best principal in our county.

—An elementary school teacher

In the preceding chapters, we discussed the strategies of praise and expectations used by effective transformational principals to influence teachers. The use of these strategies gives teachers clear feedback regarding their principals' perceptions of their classroom performance and clear knowledge of the criteria against which principals judge success.

The next several chapters describe ways that principals influence teacher commitment and effort through careful attention to their professional needs. Although decision making in schools is a complex process and different approaches are appropriate under different circumstances (see Hoy & Miskel, 2005, and Owens & Valesky, 2007 for excellent reviews of decision making models), here we specifically recount how principals described by the teachers in our study involved teachers in school-wide decisions, expanded teachers' autonomy in the areas of curriculum and instruction, and increased teachers' opportunities for professional development, all of which are essential to school improvement (Cibulka, 2001; Elmore, 2004; Fullan, 2005; Marks & Louis, 1999; Marks & Nance, 2007; Spillane, Halverson, & Diamond, 2004). The importance of shared leadership to effective school improvement has been discussed in virtually every national and state study of effective school administration (Ward & MacPhail-Wilcox, 1999). Of all the influence strategies used by effective transformational principals, our teachers identified only one other strategy—praise—more often than faculty participation.

Shared decision making, empowerment, involvement, teamwork, collaboration, participatory management, flat structures, shared governance—the terms are countless. Each year an organizational scholar adds a brighter bow, but the new packaging conceals old contents. Inside is the weapon proclaimed to fight bureaucratic inertia: participation by the workers in the governance of an organization (e.g., Conley & Bacharach, 1990; Glickman, 1993, 1998; Maeroff, 1988; Schlechty, 1990).

The rationale for school improvement goes something like this: Each school serves a unique student clientele. Therefore, top-down governance, where goals and procedures are decreed for many different schools, is bound to fail on its own. Teachers and school administrators, as professionals, are best qualified to make decisions affecting their unique student populations. Well organized and facilitated shared decision-making processes that draw on the expertise of many teacher-professionals in a given school are superior to individual decisions made by an administrator. Such processes are essential to establishing internal accountability and capacity for sustained improvement (Elmore, 2004; Fullan, 2005).

What do other researchers report about the role of teacher participation as it relates to school improvement? A group of researchers comparing high- and low-achieving California schools concludes that governance of the school's instructional program has a direct effect on student achievement. Specifically, teachers in high-achieving schools are more involved in instructional programs than teachers in low-achieving schools. Principals in low-achieving schools are more likely to profess confidence in their teachers' abilities by "leaving them alone to teach" than by granting them participation in decision making (Heck, Larsen, & Marcoulides, 1990; Heck & Marcoulides, 1993; Riordan & da Costa, 1998).

Other researchers draw similar conclusions with regard to faculty participation in successfully restructured schools focused on school improvement. Blase and Blase (2001) identify nine major strategies used by "exemplary" shared governance principals to enhance teacher empowerment and involvement in school-based decision making. Such strategies result in, for example, increases in teacher motivation, confidence, sense of ownership, reflection, commitment, risk taking, autonomy, and teaching efficacy. In other studies, these researchers learned that similar effects on teachers result when principals considered to be effective instructional leaders use a range of "collaborative" strategies to influence classroom teaching and learning (Blase & Blase, 2004; Blase & Phillips, 2008).

Researchers have also found evidence of improved student achievement, lower dropout rates, gains in teachers' critical thinking skills, and improved school climate in Georgia schools that gave teachers a voice in school governance (Allen, Glickman, & Hensley, 1998; Glickman, 1990). These outcomes are attributed to the pride that developed as a result of teacher involvement and to a new manner in which teachers viewed their work.

Our teachers reported that effective transformational principals encourage teacher participation in creating school vision, planning, choosing among alternative courses of action, and achieving agreed-upon objectives. Other studies confirm the importance of involving teachers in such aspects of school reform (e.g. Blase & Phillips, 2008; Leithwood, Chapman, Corson, Hallinger, & Hart, 1996b; Leithwood & Jantzi, 2000; Murphy & Datnow, 2003; Waters et al., 2003). Owens & Valesky (2007) point out that this process is continuous; plans are revised in light of changing developments that call into question any aspect of the process.

In recent years there has been great emphasis on using a broad range of existing data to inform continuous school improvement, including alternative assessments, portfolios, grade retention data, and high school completion data as well as data produced by use of action research at the school and classroom levels. Data are also used, for example, to develop school goals, design staff development, and evaluate effects of classroom teaching strategies on student learning (Schmuck, 2006). Blase and Phillips (2008) found that transformational principals in high-achieving schools strongly supported teachers' use of data for school improvement.

If I Have the Buck, Why Should You Get to Deal?

"The buck stops here." Harry Truman kept that reminder on his desk. In formal organizations, responsibility (and blame) rests with the person at the top of the hierarchy. Principals know that they are ultimately responsible for the outcomes of decisions made at their schools. (Very often that message is reinforced by district supervisors.) So, if principals hold the buck, why should they allow teachers to deal the cards?[1] Our data underscore several reasons for "sharing the deal": Involvement in decision making by those affected by the decisions is used to create faculty unity, to improve morale, to engender support for decisions, and, perhaps most important, to improve the quality of decisions.

Faculty Cohesiveness and Morale

According to the teachers in our study, principals often express a desire to unite their faculties through collaboration. Language is used extensively to accomplish this goal; such words as *family*, *team*, *cooperation, community, unity,* and *harmony* are employed because they convey what effective principals hope to accomplish through shared decision making. As one teacher commented, the principal involves teachers in group activities "to solidify the faculty's bonding to the school." Other principals express their interest in faculty unity through a variety of actions:

> *He encourages everyone to take part in everything.*
> *Fundraisers, field day, or a faculty party/dinner—it doesn't*
> *matter. We are representatives of Lincoln Elementary. We all*
> *play or no one plays. We're a family of devoted people. We aim,*
> *plan, and succeed.*

Closely related to the goal of faculty unity is the desire to improve teacher morale through inclusion. Participation is seen as a way to "diffuse problems that could demoralize faculty" by making "each teacher feel . . . part of the school family."

Fostering Support From Teachers

In our conversations with school administrators, we often hear the criticism that faculty empowerment reduces the power of the principal. In their version of "why should I let them deal the cards," the skeptic and the politician argue, "After all, we were hired to run the school." Indeed, this argument is a salient one, particularly if a traditional management perspective prevails.

But power is not necessarily a finite resource. Our teachers disclosed that transformational principals believe their power actually expands when it is shared. As one teacher explained, her principal seeks faculty input in decision making because "he wants ground-level support for his ideas. It's easier to support his agenda in a climate of trust and cooperation."

Kouzes and Posner (1990) concur with this view of power. In their study of the distribution of power in branch offices of a nationwide insurance company, they found that

> The leaders in the more successful branch offices understood,
> and acted on, [the belief] that "power is an expandable pie"—

that power is not a zero-sum commodity, requiring that for others to have more, the leader must have less. The more everyone in the organization feels a sense of power and influence, the greater the ownership and investment they feel in the success of the organization. (p. 164)

Blase and Blase (2001) found that principals who effectively practice shared leadership did more than share power, they "multiplied" it and produced greater capacity and leadership density in their schools. Clearly, power is expandable and reciprocal and can produce synergistic outcomes (Drake & Roe, 2003).

After reviewing myriad studies of school reform, Murphy and Datnow (2003) concluded that a principal's ability to create internal capacity and dense leadership are associated with successfully implementing deep school reform. This is especially true when people are required to produce adaptive solutions (i.e., answers to problems not known) versus simple technical solutions (i.e., solutions to challenges known) (Fullan, 2005).

The "expandability" of the power pie through shared ownership was recognized by our teachers. Our research indicates that principals who want to ensure support ("buy-in") for their policies and programs solicit teacher involvement at the early planning stages of a project, rather than mandating participation during the later stages of implementation.

Advantages of Shared Decision Making

Are decisions made by a group of teachers ultimately better decisions than those made by one or two administrators? From our data, we learned that the process of shared decision making significantly strengthens support for decisions and improves faculty morale. Still, the process is time-consuming and not without its detractors. Buck hoarding and power counting with finite numbers are not easily reversed. For administrators anxious about their own evaluations, the thought of relinquishing power while remaining unable to relinquish blame is a frightening proposition. The effective transformational principals discussed in our study, however, recognized a decided advantage to shared governance: Shared decisions are usually better than individual ones, a conclusion that also frequently appears in the general management literature (Porter, Bigley, & Steers, 2003).

Our teachers reported that their principals need teacher expertise to make informed decisions. Teachers' "formal and informal knowledge" (e.g., subject matter, expertise, and knowledge of student needs), "creative ideas," and "experience" all are valued by effective principals. Furthermore, we learned that task coverage (i.e., the number of tasks that could be accomplished) increases as a result of relying on others: "By diversifying decision making and tasks, the principal hopes to be more effective," one teacher explained.

In some cases, principals rely on teachers to compensate for their own areas of weakness. According to one teacher, "He [the principal] needs my organizing and verbal skills because he is insecure in these areas." Some readers might feel that delegation and participation are tools for less competent administrators who must cover their own shortcomings, but keep in mind that these were recognized as strategies used by very effective principals. Such school leaders apparently realize that they cannot provide effective leadership in all aspects of the school. At the Second International Congress on School Effectiveness, held in the Netherlands in 1989, Phil Hallinger argued that because of the multitude of leadership functions and the limited time available, principals (especially in high schools) should not attempt to centralize the role of instructional leader. Such restriction of involvement would reduce the likelihood of school effectiveness. Hallinger urged principals to define the specific functions and behaviors of instructional leaders, to identify their own strengths in these areas, and to delegate functions outside of their expertise to a leadership team. Instead of viewing faculty participation and delegation as confessions of their ineptitude, transformational principals should tout them as badges of their genius (Hallinger, 1989).

TEACHER EFFECTS

Attitudes Toward Involvement

Teachers in our study were excited about the opportunities offered by participatory school governance. Feelings of comfort, satisfaction, and heightened self-esteem were associated with increased involvement. When involvement took the form of participation in decision making, teachers felt especially valued and important: "I feel that what I think matters; I matter!" Teachers also felt more secure when formal structures for faculty input exist: "I feel that there is a way to channel ideas and concerns . . . there is a forum for my frustrations or trouble areas that arise."

Delegation of certain responsibilities, including extracurricular responsibilities, is another form of involvement that creates feelings of pride, inclusion, and empowerment for teachers. Terms such as *flattered*, *capable*, and *appreciated* were used to describe teachers' attitudes toward delegation. Teachers also developed a "whole-school perspective" or the ability to "see the big picture" as a result of their increased involvement. They reported becoming aware of the roles and responsibilities of others within the school and developing greater empathy for others as a result.

Teachers' overwhelming response to being involved in the school in meaningful ways was quite positive; however, a few teachers mentioned occasional negative feelings. Additional demands on their time bothered some teachers, particularly when they felt that the issues being addressed were perceived as inconsequential: "Sometimes too much time is spent on minor details." The time problem as it relates to shared leadership should not be taken lightly. At the 1990 meeting of the American Educational Research Association, educational researcher Carol Weiss revealed that in most of the schools she studied, teachers were used in an advisory capacity, and the overwhelming majority of issues addressed by school leadership teams were mundane and routine. These findings point to a basic truth: When teachers feel their time is being wasted on trivial matters, they are likely to resent involvement.

Closely related to the issue of time is the sincerity of principals who invite teachers to participate in school governance. If principals solicit teacher participation, teacher input must be reflected in the decisions ultimately made. Because faculty empowerment is such a popular notion in the school improvement literature, some administrators may obligingly implement superficial structures for shared decision making, with little intention of implementing decisions conflicting with their own preferences. They may limit faculty discretion to minor issues or they may engage teachers in time-consuming deliberations that tend to be ignored. To illustrate, one teacher in our study discussed feelings of manipulation in conjunction with her principal's use of faculty participation. Although the principal was evaluated as generally effective and his request for faculty input in key decisions was appreciated, the teacher resented his "tendency to do what he wants anyway" despite the input he received. Thus, faculty participation appears to be most effective when administrators learn to trust the decisions that ensue and when the issue at hand justifies the time expended.[2]

Other principals may be sincerely interested in implementing shared leadership but fall victim to "inadvertent domination"; this may be produced by traditional expectations of self and others and the principals' possession of information not available to others (Reitzug & Cross, 1994). Bredeson (1995) found that significant role changes for principals may produce loss of control, fear of failure, frustration, self-doubts about competency and ability to succeed, and identity loss. Beatty (2000) found that shared leadership and letting go of control resulted from experience, deliberate reflection, and successfully coping with others. Empowering principals successfully overcome such issues because of the positive effects on themselves (e.g., increase in motivation), on school decision-making processes and structures, and on teachers' professional development (Blase & Blase, 1996, 2001).

Given the difficulty in maintaining a focus on significant issues in restructured schools, Kirby's (1992) propositions are instructive with regard to effective practice:

1. Shared decision making will be more likely to address issues of greater significance when minor faculty concerns are

resolved first, thereby fostering trust in the process and facilitating a more professional culture.

2. Shared decision making will be more likely to address issues of greater significance when teachers are able to focus their own work through formal structures for goal setting, determining agendas, and reaching decisions.

3. Shared decision making will be more likely to address issues of greater significance when teachers are involved in prioritizing concerns and when those teachers declare a stake in the outcomes.

4. Shared decision making will be more likely to address issues of greater significance when the database for generating concerns, alternatives, and solutions is both comprehensive and objective (such as an analysis of optimum and existing school effectiveness criteria to generate concerns or an Internet search to generate alternatives).

Involvement and Teacher Performance

A common problem that has appeared in the reform literature is that school administrators, while using the rhetoric of shared leadership, tend to manipulate teachers to comply with their wishes (Owens & Valesky, 2007). In spite of the occasional misuses of faculty involvement, our teachers were generally satisfied with its use. The attitudes of teachers are certainly critical in determining the efficacy of any influence strategy, but of equal or greater importance are the effects on teacher behavior. Earlier we spoke of the goals that principals associate with the use of faculty involvement (e.g., faculty unity, improved morale, increased levels of support, better instructional decisions). According to our data, teachers' reactions to increased participation are consistent with their principals' intentions and serve to build a school's external capacity for school improvement. Maeroff (1993) notes that this increased capacity can help tremendously in dealing with a school's most difficult problems.

Working Harder

Teachers reported that because of the availability of avenues for participation, time and energy increasingly were devoted to various aspects of decision making. While spending more time on planning and problem solving, teachers become more careful and self-reliant because they feel ownership in and responsibility for the school's effectiveness. One teacher explained, "I act cautiously in implementing and enforcing decisions because I know my principal's and my reputation are at stake." Another remarked, "I think more to look for a solution to a problem before asking for help. . . . I am a more capable person because I force myself to look at all angles before acting."

Many of the comments of teachers regarding participation implied dedication to the "team":

- "I know others depend on me to bring back information."
- "I am more willing to compromise when we don't agree."
- "I am supportive of ideas that develop through dialogue and will implement them whether I have been directly involved in the development of the task or not."
- "When you have a chance for input, you're not so quick to blame and point the finger."
- "If people give me responsibility, I feel compelled to carry it out well. I don't want to let others down."

Teachers attributed greater commitment, honesty, collegiality, and focus to their increased sense of belonging and being needed. They viewed faculty involvement as one of the most effective influence strategies. As one teacher summarized, "I am assured that what I do here matters . . . and often actually helps."

Returning From Abilene
(Or, Strategies for Involving)

In his whimsical parable "The Abilene Paradox," Jerry Harvey (1988) tells of his family's arduous journey in sweltering heat to eat dreadful food at a nameless cafeteria in Abilene, Texas. Why embark on such a journey? Because each member of the family thought that every other member wanted to go! Harvey blames such senseless-ness in groups on the failure to "manage agreement." Very often, he claims, members of formal or informal groups do what they believe others want. Everyone else is doing exactly the same thing. Because they fail to test their assumptions regarding agreement, groups often waste valuable time and energy doing things that no one really wants to do.

Likewise, there is often "mismanagement of agreement" on the benefits of increased involvement. Privately, the principal may say, "I'd like your input but you might think I'm shirking my responsibil-ities." To themselves, teachers may refrain, "We'd like more input but she might think that we're usurping her authority." Privately, everyone agrees, yet no one acts in accordance with their prefer-ences. Harvey suggests that only through open and frank communi-cation, initiated by one or more courageous individuals, can agreement be properly managed.

At this point we want to alert the reader to the potential problem of group think (Janis, 1985). There is no doubt that group decision making can produce high quality decisions; however, a group with too much cohesion can virtually undermine decision-making pro-cesses and outcomes. "Put plainly, when smart people act in unison, poor decisions are likely to follow" (Hoy & Miskel, 2005, p. 332). To combat group think, school principals should: make available information about group think, encourage an atmosphere of open inquiry, invite members to share doubts and criticisms, assign the role of devil's advocate to some members, and solicit feedback about group decisions from individuals outside the group. It is also wise for school administrators to remain neutral during a group's deliber-ations, at least until high levels of trust have developed (Janis, 1985).

Although recognizing that agreement is a necessary first step toward increased participation, we also need to determine how we will work to achieve our purpose. Even if we agree to go somewhere, the road to Abilene may be fraught with potholes. Therefore, we offer a corollary to the problem of failing to recognize agreement. We agree with Harvey that organizational members often share the same goals without knowing it, but we also realize that goals and the strategies for achieving them are two separate issues, each offering possibilities for agreement or disagreement. Allow us to illustrate.

One author is reminded of a typical Saturday morning in July. Her children never understood the concept of "weekend." Rather than being able to relax and enjoy not having to go to school or camp, they wanted something to do. It was the middle of summer, and surely there were possibilities beyond watching Saturday morning cartoons and Mom mowing the lawn. Everyone agreed the day was hot, all were bored, and they should find something to do. But that's where agreement ended. Attempting to "share" the decision, they found themselves inundated with strategies (even though there were only three people in this family)! The beach? One vote. A drive to the mountains? One taker. Fishing? One maybe, one yes, one no. Miniature golf? One definite no. . . . This give-and-take (or was it a give and give and give and give without any takers?) lasted most of the morning, frustrating everyone. Finally, all conceded that it was too late in the day to do anything.

This scenario will be familiar to many—husbands and wives, parents and children, a group of friends, a collection of teachers. We all have encountered situations in which we agreed that we wanted to do something but could not agree on what to do or how to do it. Similarly, school faculties and administrators often agree that they want to do something about increased involvement, but they have great difficulty reaching agreement on exactly what to do and how to achieve it.

We often ask students in our school leadership course to describe their concept of an empowered school. Because the majority of graduate students are practicing teachers and aspiring administrators, they are aware of the research supporting shared governance in schools. Most often (at least in the safe setting of the university), agreement on this issue is managed without having to take the trip to Abilene. But our students are constantly amazed at the sheer number of issues that remain to be resolved even after they agree on the advantages of shared decision making. They grapple with questions such as:

- Who will be directly involved in making decisions—all teachers or a representative committee?
- If a representative committee is used, how will members be chosen? How long will they serve?
- What role will the principal and other administrators have in making decisions? Will they have an equal vote? No vote? Veto power?
- What issues are open to the process of shared decision making? Are any excluded?
- Who determines which issues will be addressed by the decision-making body?
- How are decisions ultimately reached? Majority vote? Consensus? Unanimous approval?
- Once decisions are made, who actually carries them out?

Not surprisingly, no two groups of students ever have created identical structures for faculty involvement. Many factors contribute to this: the proportion of teachers to administrators in the group, personal assumptions of group members (e.g., their views on power and authority), past experiences with shared governance, knowledge of possible governance structures gained through readings or training, and the level of creativity of the group. We should expect the same in actual schools. If schools are indeed idiosyncratic, it is unlikely that different schools would adopt the exact same structure for faculty involvement. In fact, Glickman (1990) cautions that one irony of empowerment is that "the more an empowered school becomes a model of success, the less the school becomes a practical model to be imitated by others" (p. 71). It seems that if a collection of individuals agrees to make decisions about where to go and how to get there, the individuals are obliged first to decide how they will decide. Using a decision made by any other group (i.e., adopting an existing model) negates the very first decision—agreeing to make decisions for themselves.

This rather lengthy introduction to involving others is intended as a cautionary note to those reading this chapter with hopes of answering the question, "How can I effectively involve faculty in decision making?" The truth of the matter is that transformational principals do it in many different ways.[3] We offer the variations to be used, not in imitation, but in bits and pieces, to be pondered, remolded, and adapted wherever appropriate.

Formal Strategies for Involvement

Our data indicate that faculty involvement in decision making is most extensive when formal team structures are in place. Although the majority of principals who use involvement as an influence strategy do not themselves create such structures, those who do are perceived as much more effective. Those principals tend to involve more people and to concede more authority on a wider range of issues related to school empowerment.

We found that a variety of team structures are discussed and various designations are used—professional involvement committee, school climate committee, advisory council of teachers, and leadership management team. Formal teams generally convene regularly, usually once a week. Team members are chosen most frequently on the basis of their roles in the school. Second-level administrators (e.g., department chairpersons, grade-level coordinators, counselors) seemed to make up most of the teams noted in our study. In some cases, teachers with no administration or coordination responsibilities also were included on the leadership teams. Other staff members, such as cafeteria administrators, were involved when appropriate.

Teachers who do not have opportunities to be on leadership teams tend to be involved in decisions on a more limited basis. They are expected to make suggestions to their team representatives either orally or in writing. In effect, their ideas could reach the team's agenda if activated through these channels.

For faculty members on leadership teams—either because of their other roles in the school or because of certain appointments or elections—involvement and effect are more direct. We found that teams usually assume a problem-identification/problem-solving orientation. Some teams focused almost entirely on problems identified by the principal, whereas others participated fully in identifying problems and developing solutions.

Teams address a broad range of problems. According to one teacher:

> *All faculty members have the opportunity to give input by writing their concerns on a list posted on the "sign-in" counter in the office. No problem or concern is too small. Anything and everything listed on the agenda is discussed and answered.*

Many of the teams noted in our study attempted to respond to a range of issues. School climate, curriculum, student discipline, scheduling, faculty morale, parental involvement, and fundraising and school improvement were among the many problems resolved by representative leadership teams. A stream of studies confirms that teams emphasizing school improvement can influence student achievement (Marzano, Waters, & McNulty, 2005).

Our data also suggest that formal authority for making decisions sometimes rests with the leadership teams. More often—in roughly 60 percent of the cases—teams served in an advisory capacity. According to one teacher, the principal "reserves decision making as an administrative prerogative; sometimes suggestions are implemented, other times they are not."

Informal and Impromptu Involving

Our teachers reported that informal participation opportunities also provide legitimate channels for them to express their thoughts and feelings on a range of personal and professional issues. Principals often endorse an open-door policy to encourage teachers to express their problems and concerns freely. Impromptu encounters with teachers are used to solicit input on a variety of problems. In addition, faculty meetings are conducted in a relaxed and open manner, allowing teachers the freedom to voice their concerns and to develop solutions collaboratively. Occasionally, faculty meetings are scheduled in response to problems that surface. In effect, teacher input is solicited during scheduled faculty meetings and during both scheduled and chance individual meetings. In an overwhelming majority of high performance schools studied by Blase and Phillips (2008), faculty meetings were called only when collaboration was required specifically for whole school improvement.

Where no formal structure for faculty involvement exists, the faculty's role tends to be advisory only: Teachers give opinions, and principals make decisions. Nevertheless, teachers in our study were pleased that informal channels for participation allowed them input on many different issues.

Delegation is another informal involvement tactic used by effective principals. Whereas formal and informal meetings often are used for planning and generating alternative solutions to problems, delegation is used to inspire action. Here, principals are seen as extending varying degrees of authority and responsibility to teachers to resolve problems that surface or to handle extracurricular activities. Teachers are selected for their expertise or for special qualities such as loyalty and pride. The selection of teachers by principals to assume added duties conveys confidence, which motivates teachers:

My principal asked me to be in charge of organizing the work necessary for participation in the School of Excellence Program. Knowing the vast amount of writing that must be done, he chose me because I am an English teacher and a good organizer. I am flattered. I love a good challenge.

We should mention that the teachers who participated in the study on which this book is based have not been empowered fully. Although many teachers are involved in some capacity in the decisions made in their schools, few principals actually relinquished a significant degree of authority. Still, teachers tell us that the involvement they have is preferable to none at all.

SUGGESTIONS FOR EFFECTIVE INVOLVEMENT

Again we must caution that a laundry list of dos and don'ts for effective involvement borders on hypocrisy. We cannot suggest the best team structure or the right distribution of authority or the most important activities to delegate; shared decision making means that the principal along with others must decide those issues. Other researchers found that establishment of a shared vision, consistent policies regarding delegation, risk taking, nurturing, and an educational rather than technical emphasis are mechanisms used by good principals to involve teachers (Rosenblum, Louis, & Rossmiller, 1994). From our research, we add these suggestions for facilitating faculty involvement.

1. Manage agreement.

   Before instituting formal or informal mechanisms for involving faculty in planning and decision making, principals must assess their own and their faculty's desire and readiness to undertake such an arrangement. The concepts of power and responsibility should be discussed openly; involvement will remain untried if lack of agreement is assumed. Change can begin when those involved in decision making risk discovering where agreement exists.

2. Involve individuals.

   Effective principals create a climate for participation by delegating responsibility to willing teachers who have the relevant knowledge and skill, and providing professional development opportunities for all to develop such knowledge and skill related to conflict, communication, problem solving, and data analysis, among others.

3. Use every opportunity to involve informally.

   Effective principals involve others by inviting free expression of suggestions, advice, concerns, and problems. Among the available forums they use for soliciting teacher input are faculty meetings, chance encounters, open door, and scheduled meetings with individuals or groups.

4. Encourage formal mechanisms for involvement.

    Effective principals assist teachers in developing formal channels for faculty participation. When formal structures exist, teachers are routinely more involved and are more active in school governance. Formal structures must be created at the school level that reflect the unique realities of a given school context.

5. Know when not to involve.

    Effective principals increase faculty involvement because they expect positive results—perhaps improved morale, better decisions, or efficiency. If a decision that involves many people is expected to achieve the same or inferior outcomes as a decision made alone, the decision probably should be made alone. In the long run, teachers resent involvement on trivial matters. Such involvement will be seen as a waste of valuable time.

6. Respect the decisions of the team.

    Regardless of the particular structure for faculty participation, effective principals value decisions that are made collectively. As such, they view themselves as members of the team—they are willing to share responsibility for dealing the cards and are willing to play the cards that are dealt.

7. Emphasize continuous school improvement.

    Involvement in decision making by teachers is most likely to produce effects on teaching and student learning where collaboration focuses on school improvement.

8. Emphasize the use of data for school improvement.

    For data to be useful in improving a school, principals and teachers must have professional development about assessment. Unfortunately, pre-service preparation of principals and teachers regarding assessment is too often weak or nonexistent, so they must be provided with extensive opportunities to gain knowledge and develop skills in formative assessment, data collection, data analysis, and data-driven instructional planning and evaluation.

NOTES

1. The phrase *pass the buck* is believed to have originated in poker games, when a buckhorn-handled knife ("buck," for short) was used to designate the next player to deal a jackpot game.

2. We recognize that teachers also contribute to the success or failure of shared decision making. Weiss (1990) suggests that teachers themselves often choose to spend time on trivial issues because those issues are more familiar and less threatening. Development of teacher attitudes toward, and skill in, shared governance is certainly essential to its success.

3. For an overview of four models of shared governance in schools and the effectiveness of each in empowering teachers, see Hallinger and Richardson (1988).

CHAPTER FIVE

Granting Professional Autonomy

The principal in my school supports his faculty and treats each member as a professional. He gives his teachers the freedom to teach without harassment. He is adept at hiring the kind of teacher who works well with students and other teachers. He then leaves the teaching to those who are trained, providing support when it's needed. I would find it demeaning and unsatisfying to work under the restraints imposed by many other principals. This man knows what to do to get the most from his teachers.

—An elementary school teacher

In this chapter we discuss an influence strategy that is frequently misunderstood: granting professional autonomy. A straightforward definition of autonomy is followed by a brief discussion of its importance to teacher motivation, commitment, and school improvement as well as its place in hindering versus enabling school bureaucracies. A discussion of the difference between "freedom from" and "freedom to" provides the necessary platform for understanding the kind of autonomy emphasized by effective transformational principals. At the same time, we argue that teacher autonomy is naturally influenced by federal, state, and school district policy as well as by a principal's use of other influence strategies (e.g., expectations) discussed in this book.

Within professional school organizations, workers value autonomy in decision making. Colleagues serve as the reference group for evaluating choices, standards of control are self-imposed, and a professional code of ethics guides decisions. Within strictly bureaucratic structures, teachers' actions are judged against their conformity to rules, regulations, and expectations held by superiors; these are referred to as hindering school structures (i.e., a hierarchy and a system of rules and regulations that impedes rather than enables teachers). The goal of hindering school structures is forced compliance of teachers (Hoy & Sweetland, 2001). Not surprisingly, authority clashes abound with teachers who value professional expertise and demand respect.

Autonomy refers to the degree of freedom (i.e., professional discretion) that individuals have in determining work processes. By virtue of their expectations for professional status, teachers demand autonomy regarding curriculum and instructional decisions, particularly at the classroom level. Time use, resource allocation, methods of instruction, and procedures for student evaluation are some processes that teachers desire to influence. Such demands by teachers are consistent with "enabling" school structures in which hierarchical authority and rules and regulations are viewed as guides to problem solving and school improvement, and used to support teachers who work collaboratively—across authority lines—with administrators (Hoy & Sweetland, 2001).

Teacher autonomy is an important aspect of teacher work motivation and a key factor in school reform (Short, 1994); it is also positively linked to teacher behaviors that foster student learning (Hoy & Miskel, 2005). Teacher autonomy can be an important moderator of job-related stress (Spector, 2002), and it is positively related to commitment, satisfaction, and work adjustment (Aryee & Stone, 1996; Bhuian, Al-Shammari, & Jefri, 1996). Pearson and Moomaw (2005) found that increases in teacher autonomy are related to decreases in job-related stress and increases in satisfaction, as well as perceived empowerment and professionalism. In general, autonomy is considered a basic human need necessary for optimal functioning and growth (Ryan & Deci, 2003). Unfortunately, it may also be one of teachers' greatest deficiencies (see, for example, Nero, 1985).

The formal position held by principals in school organizations is assumed by many to give them authority to influence behavior in schools. Teachers typically separate the educational function from the management function in acknowledging principals' authority, however. Teachers are willing to accept principals' authority in scheduling, public relations, and student services. In contrast, in the realm of instruction, teachers claim the authority of expertise and assert that this professional authority supersedes the principal's positional authority. This *authority paradox* (Donaldson, 1990) makes the instructional leadership role currently advocated in much of the school reform and improvement literature difficult for school administrators to enact.

Hoy and Miskel (2005) assert that autonomy is undeniable in schools due to the physical isolation of teachers in their classrooms, the relatively infrequent opportunities for administrators to monitor teachers' work, and the broad authority teachers have over student activities. Although it may be true that autonomy at the classroom level is difficult to deny, there is great variability among schools in the amount of autonomy principals grant teachers regarding schoolwide issues. In one study of decision participation, it was found that teachers wanted more discretion in every decision area investigated, including school and classroom assignments, facilities planning, how and what to teach, and staff development (Bacharach, Bamberger, Conley, & Bauer, 1990). In other studies, teacher autonomy, individual and group, focused on teaching and learning and factors that directly and indirectly affect school improvement (Blase & Blase, 1996, 2001, 2004; Blase & Phillips, 2008). In our opinion, robust approaches to teacher autonomy that focus on school improvement are more powerful and effective.

FREEDOM FROM AND FREEDOM TO

Rosenholtz (1989) further distinguishes between two kinds of autonomy in schools: freedom *from* and freedom *to*. She found that where teacher commitment and collaboration are low, teachers are more concerned with "freedom from." They are bored, helpless, and defensive. Constructing their own version of autonomy, teachers escape from such conditions with frequent absences. By contrast, teachers who are given frequent opportunities for learning and collaboration are more committed to their students and feel a freedom to grow and develop that has few limitations. Our teachers also alluded to both kinds of freedoms in their schools. They associated principal effectiveness with wide discretion in instruction and curriculum (i.e., freedom to) as well as with lack of intrusion and intervention (i.e., freedom from).

The Inspection Taboo

Rosenholtz (1989) refers to the desire of teachers in what she calls "stuck" schools to escape from the boredom and frustration of their everyday work conditions. Some teachers view this control as a form of power over their lives. In our study, we found that teachers associated freedom from close inspection with autonomy. They reasoned that because they are professionals, they are self-monitoring. Administrators, like office managers in a medical complex, are not to intrude in the professional realm. One teacher reported:

[My principal] allows me to conduct my classroom as I see fit. He doesn't give unwanted advice and has never tried to "take over" my classroom. . . . I think I do a better job as a result of not being hassled.

Meyer and Rowan (1977) argue that school administrators do avoid intrusion into the instructional realm. They attribute this avoidance to structural and psychological barriers rather than to their belief in the true professionalism of teachers. Because of the "loose coupling" (e.g., between teachers, subject areas, departments, and grade levels) characteristic of school organizations, teachers are afforded a high degree of autonomy. Allowing teachers to remain autonomous (i.e., not closely supervising them) gives the appearance of legitimizing their professional status. Also, if principals supervise more closely, they risk uncovering defects in practice—defects that would require correction. Given that there is little certainty regarding what constitutes effective practice, principals are reluctant to confront teachers with accusations of ineffective practice. Thus, principals benefit from perpetuating what Meyer and Rowan call a "myth of professionalism." With increasing demands for accountability and instructional leadership in schools, it is not surprising that principals have denied that they purposely limit inspection of teachers (Okeafor & Teddlie, 1989). Nonetheless, teachers often associate avoidance with professional autonomy.

Our data suggest that the "freedom from" dimension of autonomy is not an overarching concern of teachers who rate their principals as effective transformational leaders. These teachers, however, do convey an expectation that principals should involve themselves in classroom practices in a positive, constructive, nonjudgmental, and supportive manner. Likewise, Goldman, Dunlap, and Conley (1991) report that principals involved in one reform project saw their role not as interfering with teachers in their improvement efforts, but as helping them clear the way, particularly by making time available for teacher collaboration. More specifically, in studies of teacher empowerment and shared decision making, Blase and Blase (1996, 2001, 2004) and Blase and Phillips (2008) found that successful principals encourage teacher autonomy by using strategies such as demonstrating trust, developing shared decision-making structures, encouraging innovation and risk taking, soliciting teachers' input, and buffering instructional time from interruptions.

Closer analysis of our data reveals, however, that teacher autonomy is significantly delimited. State and local policies and practices limit teacher discretion, but principals' expectations and advice also reduce teacher latitude in decision making. Although teachers associate autonomy with professionalism, they acknowledge limitations and the need for exceptions. Teachers stated:

- "She allows each teacher the freedom to teach within his/her own style, recognizing individual differences as long as we stay within the guidelines of the school philosophy."

- "He treats us as professionals . . . tells us the end results he expects . . . keeps us informed about what needs to be done . . . and leaves the many details to our discretion."

Thus, there did not seem to be an implicit assumption among these teachers that principals had no authority in the realm of instruction.

Teachers explained that because their principals were deemed effective on a number of dimensions, their advice and expectations were accepted. There is evidence that principals who demonstrate expertise in the areas of curriculum and instruction engender greater loyalty and satisfaction among teachers. Indeed, the amount of inspection and the limitations placed on work that is acceptable to teachers seem to be related to the professional respect that teachers hold for their principals' expertise. "Freedom from" may be of greater concern to teachers who work with less effective principals.

Autonomy: Freedom To

The most important aspect of autonomy for our teachers appears to be the freedom to teach in ways that teachers deem most effective. Teachers expressed strong convictions that they should be allowed to make decisions regarding what and how they teach. They reported that effective transformational principals grant them such authority:

- "I teach the information that I feel is more important."
- "I am at liberty to be an individual and use my own teaching techniques."

On the surface, granting autonomy seems to be a fairly straight-forward technique: Teachers are given professional discretion regarding curriculum and instruction, at least within their own class-rooms. Many teachers reported that principals modify autonomy in subtle ways, however. It is important to keep in mind that individual principals use many of the strategies reported in this book. Autonomy is nearly always used in conjunction with other influence strategies. Principals moderate their use of authority by conveying expectations for teacher performance. Further moderation results from involvement of groups of teachers in schoolwide decisions. Principals also extend professional autonomy to groups of teachers (as well as to individuals) who are entrusted with critical decisions, as reported by teachers in our study. Finally, principals influence curriculum and instruction by disseminating information regarding effective teaching practices and student learning, and by suggesting strategies for improvement.

Ackerman, Donaldson, and van der Bogert (1996) argue further that responsibility for instructional supervision must be fully shared by teachers and principals alike. Following their suggestion, in the realm of curriculum and instruction, principals might increase teachers' collective autonomy by sharing accountability for teaching as a whole. Individual autonomy would be less valued. Support for teachers' involvement in the supervision of instruction is found also in reviews of the knowledge base for school learning that conclude emphasis on proximal variables such as curriculum and instruction has greater influence on student learning than emphasis on distal variables such as school-based decision making (Wang, Haertel, & Walberg, 1993).

In a recent study of emergent teacher leadership (i.e., naturally-occurring, informal, and spontaneous collaboration among teachers, a form of teacher autonomy), Blase and Blase (2006) found that teachers provided significant support to colleagues by promoting caring and building trust, consulting about the formal knowledge base, helping colleagues plan and organize for learning, modeling appropriate classroom behavior, and guiding classroom management. Outcomes of informal teacher leadership included increases in the use of effective teaching and learning strategies and teachers' ability to meet diverse student needs, as well as increases in teachers' efficacy and continuing commitment to professional growth. Blase and Blase advise principals to support informal teacher leadership by providing recognition and appreciation for such efforts as well as developing professional learning communities, which they reported spawned informal collaboration among teachers.

Benefits of Changing the Myth to Reality

Whether professionalism in teaching is fact or myth, the benefits of treating teachers as professionals are indisputable. In spite of autonomy's somewhat tempered use, our study indicates that extending autonomy to teachers has overall positive effects on attitudes and performance. Teachers reported that autonomy makes them feel "proud," "professional," "confident," "competent," "trusted," and "free." Some disclosed that they became more reflective and creative in resolving classroom difficulties:

- "When I'm in a difficult situation . . . I can reflect on how a professional would handle it and follow through on my own."
- "I am encouraged and feel free to use my design and problem-solving skills."

Some teachers indicated that they conform to principals' expectations because principals respect their opinions and feelings. Others reported working harder and longer. Most felt that autonomy is deserved and essential:

- "A teacher doesn't need to feel timid about the use of their [sic] freedom and power."
- "I have the personality that does not like to be told what to do on issues that I see as my domain."

Numerous studies reveal similar outcomes for teachers working with other transformational school principals (Blase & Blase, 1996 2001, 2004; Blase & Phillips, 2008; Leithwood, 1994). Like the principals described in our study, transformational principals are able to strike a balance between encouraging professional autonomy and the need for professional oversight.

Only one teacher expressed some confusion resulting from the use of autonomy. His remarks demonstrate the mixed messages that can result when more direction from principals is desired. This suggests that the degree of autonomy granted must be appropriately matched to the ability and desire of the teacher:

I feel gratitude and anger. I appreciate the opportunity to think about school improvement. I sometimes feel frustrated and angered by my isolation, lack of direction, and the assumption that I'll get it done.

IMPLICATIONS FOR PRACTICE

We must take great caution in offering suggestions to use autonomy to influence teacher behavior. The term *autonomy* is interpreted differently in different settings and by different teachers. The degree of autonomy can range from a high degree of freedom in a broad range of issues to limited discretion over defined issues in particular settings. Even when techniques are defined, the effects may vary from one teacher to another. Ever mindful of these constraints, we ask the reader to consider the following carefully.

1. Emphasize what is meant by autonomy. Emphasize freedom *to*, not freedom *from*.

   Be sure that teachers understand that they are given freedom to make decisions regarding curriculum and instruction. Explain whether that authority extends beyond the classroom. Insist that autonomy does not mean freedom from all forms of monitoring or supervision. In professional organizations, the autonomous are also accountable. (Of course, using Rosenholtz's [1989] definition there is an accompanying freedom from boredom and isolation.)

2. Emphasize that autonomy is extended out of a sense of professionalism and trust. It is not an abdication of authority.

   Some teachers resent the principal who fails to become involved in any capacity in decisions regarding instruction. By virtue of their expertise in pedagogy as well as administration, principals too can claim the status of professional educators. They should offer advice when asked and intervene when individual problems are detected. They should never equate teacher autonomy with laissez faire leadership.

3. Use other influence strategies in conjunction with autonomy.

   Granting professional autonomy alone can be a very passive means of influencing teacher performance. Effective transformational principals combine this strategy with other, more proactive, strategies—such as conveying expectations, involving groups of teachers in schoolwide decisions, providing professional literature related to improvement, providing opportunities for professional development, and supporting formal and informal approaches to teacher collaboration and professional learning community.

4. Assess individual readiness for autonomy.

   Whereas some teachers are offended by overtly directive and intrusive principals, others resent the nondirective or facilitative approach. For these teachers, and particularly for novices, feedback about performance should be frequent and semi-prescriptive. The need for individual assistance should be assessed regularly through conferences with teachers and through informal classroom observations.

CHAPTER SIX

Leading by Standing Behind

A parent called my principal to complain that his child had been given a test that was different from the other students' tests. My principal then called me to his office, explained that a parent had made a complaint, and proceeded to gather details from me. . . . He was concerned about the rights of the parent, the student, and the teacher. He listened to each. . . . After I explained fully my method and reason for testing groups of students, he pointed out solutions as well as gave praise for my being a concerned teacher. The principal then called the parent and explained what we had discussed. The parent called back and asked the principal to thank me for what I was doing in the classroom.

—A middle school teacher

In Chapter 4, we suggest specific techniques for involving teachers in setting school goals and the efficacy of those techniques in influencing teacher performance. Glickman, Gordon, and Ross-Gordon (2004) review theories of adult learning and motivation to inform their developmental approach to supervision of instruction. Within the context of the school, they contend, teacher development is enhanced by linking innovations to teachers' past experiences and providing teachers the time and support needed to learn about the innovation. These authors found that the "isolations, psychological dilemma, and lack of a shared technical culture" in schools mitigate adult learning (p. 75). Interestingly, factors that we found to relate to adult learning also are related to improved student outcomes as described in a major synthesis of the best research on factors that increase student learning (Wang, Haertel, & Walberg, 1993). Transformational principals in our study enhanced teacher capacity through direct assistance in four areas: provision of the material and financial resources necessary to teach, support for teachers in the area of student discipline, protection of allocated instructional time, and reward for teachers' efforts. In short, they are perceived as effective leaders because they understand that "leading" also means "standing behind."

MATERIAL AND FINANCIAL SUPPORT

A critical component of leading by standing behind is the provision of fundamental resources. The careful selection and assignment of teachers to classes is unquestioningly a critical leadership function in effective schools, but the assignment of resources for teachers to perform their duties is equally important (Hord, 1988). Several independent research studies have associated the principal's resource-provider role with positive effects on classroom teaching and student learning (see, e.g., Ackerman, Donaldson, & van der Bogert, 1996; Andrews & Soder, 1987; Blase & Blase, 2004; Colvin, 2007; Murphy & Louis, 1994). In spite of these findings, schools and teachers all too often are judged on the basis of student outcomes, with little regard for the differences in resources available to individual schools or teachers. Ironically, new teachers—those most in need of direct assistance—are often least likely to receive the raw materials necessary to teach (Kirby, Stringfield, Teddlie, & Wimpelberg, 1992; Worthy, 2005).

Few schools offer teachers appreciable funds for the purchase of supplementary instructional materials or supplies. It is not uncommon for public school teachers to lack basic resources such as textbooks and paper. A graduate student lamented to one of the authors of this study that paper was strictly rationed at the middle school where he taught. He was allowed to make only 150 copies per week (exactly one page of paper per student!) in spite of the fact that weekly tests were encouraged and teachers were expected to send newsletters to parents on a regular basis.

Not surprisingly, our data suggest that transformational principals recognize that improved teacher performance and professional growth are more likely to occur when basic materials are available. These principals ensure that teachers have ample textbooks, paper, and equipment to teach the required curriculum. Orientation sessions acquaint new teachers with available resources and encourage their use. Supplementary materials and financial support are used to encourage innovation. Because school improvement efforts often depend on new materials and training in new methods, more effective principals support the usual rhetoric for change with the tools and training to accomplish it. One teacher wrote:

> *Time is a critical element in any school improvement effort. My principal provides me, and other teachers I work with, with almost unlimited "release" time to meet, plan, work out problems, and attend workshops. Even though half my work day is already dedicated to school improvement tasks, he is always more than willing to arrange for a substitute for my classes or those of my colleagues.*

Teachers reported several positive consequences of receiving material and financial support for instruction and professional growth. They participated in a greater number of professional seminars and applied their new knowledge to the classroom. They reported feeling more "appreciated" and "encouraged" when given access to new resources, and were more reflective on how they used resources. Their support of school improvement programs increased; as one teacher stated, "With financial support I could see that I had access to the means of participation in improvement programs. It eliminated the old hang-up of enthusiasm [about the project] without means of accomplishment."

The specific kinds of resource support that teachers in the study associated with effective principals included tuition for conferences and seminars, substitute teachers to allow regular faculty to attend conferences, basic and supplemental instructional materials, and instructional improvement grants. In some cases, funds were allotted in response to teacher requests; however, many principals were more proactive and anticipated teacher needs. Some were quite active in their pursuit of external resources:

> *As a means to help the faculty achieve the schoolwide goal of increased student success, [my principal] and his assistant principals, with other staff members, applied for and won a $95,000 grant to be used to improve instructional techniques that would help students achieve greater success in the classroom. This was a deliberate effort to show that the principal would obtain the means by which the faculty could achieve its goal.*

SUPPORT IN STUDENT DISCIPLINE

Early school-effectiveness research associated student achievement with an orderly and safe environment conducive to learning (Edmonds, 1979). More recent researchers have identified leader behaviors that enable a more studious atmosphere. Among these are high expectations for student achievement (Heck, Larsen, & Marcoulides; 1990; Heck & Marcoulides, 1993) and "backing up" teachers on matters of student discipline (Blase & Blase, 2004; Wang et al., 1993). We found principals' willingness to support (or stand behind) teachers in their decisions regarding classroom management to be a powerful form of influence over teacher behaviors and attitudes.

Because classroom management is a frequent source of frustration for teachers, effective principals work to develop teachers' classroom management skills and support their decisions in disciplinary matters. Reasons why principals support teachers' discipline strategies go beyond desires to enhance morale, however. Teachers report that transformational principals also recognize that support increases teachers' confidence ("[My principal] gives us the security to act on our own convictions"), which, in turn, increases their effectiveness in classroom management. These principals know that time expended on discipline reduces time available for instruction.

Principals also seek reductions in classroom discipline problems to improve credibility with the public: "Well-behaved students create a positive image for the school."

Teachers told us, without exception, that principal support in matters of discipline results in feelings of "confidence," "security," and "control." The following excerpts from teachers' accounts reveal that these positive outcomes are attributed to the consistency and timeliness with which principals deal with discipline matters and to principals' support of teachers when conflicts arise with parents:

- "Students know exactly what is expected. Our principal's actions support his words."
- "He always listens to the problems you have with a student, then reacts immediately through some form of disciplinary action."
- "When being accused by a parent, I know I will be supported by [my principal]. . . . Even though I may have done something wrong, I'm not belittled in front of a parent."

Teachers report working harder and accomplishing more in their classrooms because of the support they receive. Their classroom management skills improve as they adopt their principals' policy of clear expectations and consistent enforcement of rules:

- "He tells me to just tell students what is expected and then to hold them to that expectation. . . . Stick to what I say, be firm, and I will gain their respect."
- "I am less willing to bend the rules."

Some teachers report developing more positive approaches to discipline:

- "I work more diligently to maintain discipline. I have come to think of this as an important part of education."
- "I spend more time seeking the positive side of each student."

Finally, and perhaps most important, teachers believe that they are more effective because discipline issues become less stressful:

- "I don't have to lose my temper when a child refuses to behave. I can go to the office for help."
- "I can do a more effective job if I don't have to tolerate disruptive students. I look forward to going to work."

How do transformational principals support teachers' discipline efforts? In our study, support apparently began with the development of a formal schoolwide discipline program. Principals collaborated with teachers to develop and implement fair and consistent policies. Some principals provided time for teachers to participate in assertive discipline programs. The effects of such approaches are obvious in the remarks of this teacher:

> One of the strategies which has been emphasized at our elementary school is the assertive discipline approach. This approach allows the teacher to be assertive and positive. . . . With the type of students our school has, this strategy has proven to be very effective because our students are conditioned to hearing unpleasant remarks about themselves. . . . This strategy allows me to be positive. I feel like I have been changed as a teacher.

On an individual basis, principals assist teachers with student discipline by listening, giving advice, and solving problems. They constantly stress the need for clear expectations for student conduct and for consistency and fairness when dealing with disruptive students. When conflicts arise with parents, principals publicly support their teachers and help to solve problems. One principal has a policy of allowing teachers to bring parents to her office to finish conferences that appear to be getting out of control. Although a teacher reported that she had to take only one parent to the principal's office, she appreciated "the security of the principal's assistance . . . in these difficult situations." More indirectly, principals support teachers by their visibility in the school, particularly in the hallways.

PROTECTING INSTRUCTIONAL TIME

Safire and Safir (1990) tell the story of Charlie Grimm, coach of the unsuccessful Chicago Cubs in the 1930s and 1940s. Approached by an excited recruiter who had just seen a pitcher strike out 27 batters, allowing only one foul, Grimm rejected the young recruiter's desire to extend an attractive offer to the pitcher. Instead, he instructed, "Sign up the guy who got the foul. We're looking for hitters" (p. 14).

Similarly, our data indicate that effective principals understand that the key to improving their schools' effectiveness lies not with persons skilled in compliance with bureaucratic rules and procedures or in discussions about those rules, but in effective use of time allocated for instruction. In spite of pressures to maintain records and meet reporting deadlines, they recognize that what they need are teachers, not bureaucrats. Thus, a third strategy used by effective principals to increase instructional time and improve teacher morale is the deliberate reduction of extraneous demands on teachers' time. They give teachers time to teach.

Principals deemed effective in our study are aggressive in reducing interferences for teachers in two areas: paperwork and meetings. Compliance with state and federal standards has greatly increased the amount of paperwork required in schools over the last two decades. Teachers, frustrated by the additional demands on their time, are most responsive to principals who engage in actions to limit paperwork. Although the principals are unable to eliminate paperwork entirely, teachers express appreciation at their principals' concern:

> An abundance of paperwork is causing teacher burnout, stress, and negative attitudes toward our profession. Our principal (whenever possible) tries to reduce the amount of paperwork we must do. I appreciate this and try to do my job as best I can.

The principals also reinforce the value they place on instructional and planning time by limiting the number of faculty meetings. Whenever possible, they conduct informal meetings with individuals or small groups rather than with the whole faculty.

Attempts to reduce interference have a positive effect on teacher attitude, which is linked to teacher performance. One teacher noted that she is more effective because she feels more relaxed: "I don't feel pressured or under stress. I am able to work harder and get the job done."

Protection of instructional time has been found to be an important form of influence on teacher behavior in other studies as well (see, e.g., Heck et al., 1990; Heck & Marcoulides, 1993). Joyce and Showers (1995) found, however, that teacher innovation is possible only when teachers who try new practices are released from competing demands on their time. With regard to meetings, Hord (1988) warns that what teachers need is "more time for instruction and less for 'instructions'" (p. 9). Hord (1997) found that valuing and protecting instructional time is a key element of principals' leadership behavior in professional learning communities.

TANGIBLE INCENTIVES

In 1983, David Parks wrote,

> One of the most perplexing problems facing educational leaders in a period of austerity is how to maintain the cooperation and performance of a group of demoralized professionals. How does one compensate professionals for inadequate books and supplies, large classes, disruptive students, public criticism, limited assistance, increased duties, and the lowest salaries paid to highly educated personnel in the nation? How does one lead a group in which morale is so low that over 40% of survey respondents would not again select teaching as a profession and 57% are definitely planning to leave, will leave if something better comes along, or are undecided about staying? (p. 11)

Over two decades later, little has changed. Foster (2001; ¶5) wrote of one novice teacher's experience for the *Stanford Alumni Magazine*,

[Garcia-Lopez] didn't become a teacher for the money—nobody does. Like most who enter the profession, she is there for the kids, and the 60-hour workweeks are part of the gig. But Garcia-Lopez won't provide four-star service at McDonald's prices forever. And if she is like a growing number of young teachers, the poor salary will be just one variable in a yearly conundrum: to stay or to go. Energy waning, frustration growing, many will decide to leave, and in their places will come another crop of recent graduates, full of spark and dreams of changing students' lives, willing to live modestly. At least for a while.

Both Parks (1983) and Foster (2001) offer recommendations for motivating teachers in times of austerity. A more attractive work environment and intangible rewards such as recognition are among Park's prescriptions. Nevertheless, he cautions that such intangibles could serve only as temporary substitutes for tangible rewards.

We found that even in times of austerity, many principals bolster teachers' spirits by providing tangible rewards. Although the goals associated with such rewards are sometimes performance related, more often principals use rewards to improve morale and reduce absenteeism. Thus, unlike praise, which is usually tied to specific accomplishments, principals reward teachers by celebrating events such as holidays, birthdays, homecoming, and in-service days.

Some leadership theories suggest that extra effort or extraordinary performance is unrelated to such extrinsic rewards, but they recognize that ordinary performance and satisfaction are connected to the stipulations of the work contract (see, e.g., Bass, 1990). Performance—at least at some minimal level—is given in exchange for tangible rewards.

With only one exception, we found that teachers were motivated by tangible incentives. Teachers even claimed that rewards encourage innovation and extra effort beyond the confines of the classroom. Some teachers reported that they work specifically to achieve awards. Only one teacher expressed negative feelings about her principal's use of tangible incentives: "He does not believe that I as a professional will come to work because of internal motivation. I resent that." For some readers, the use of rewards may seem patronizing. The sincerity

and genuineness of the principal may be essential to the acceptabil-
ity of the strategy. Principals who use tangible incentives may positively influence teachers because they are also honest, caring, and
nonmanipulative. As one teacher whose remarks more closely
approximate the majority view pointed out: "[Rewards] show us
that the principal cares."

Because educators appear to be "stuck" in austerity, it is not surprising that tangible incentives dispensed by principals were of little
monetary significance to the teachers in our study. Food was the most
frequently discussed incentive. Some principals serve coffee and
doughnuts at staff meetings; others order breakfast or lunch for teachers on professional development days. One teacher reported that her
principal cooked a steak dinner for the whole faculty. Buttons, pins,
and ribbons are used to recognize teachers on special occasions. Shirts
with school logos are awarded for special accomplishments. Corsages
are presented to teachers at homecoming events.

Some principals sponsor social events to build morale. These
go beyond the usual office Christmas party; one more creative principal, for example, holds an ice cream party on St. Patrick's Day.
Occasionally, principals compensate for their inability to dispense
monetary rewards by giving certificates entitling teachers to arrive
late or leave early. These are tied to specific accomplishments such
as perfect attendance, for which some teachers are given half-day-
off certificates.

Foster (2001) agrees that tangible awards are necessary to retain
bright young teachers: "Particularly in traditional public schools,
teachers become frustrated by poor salaries, little administrative
support, bureaucratic decision making, and discipline problems.
They chafe at state policies and curriculum mandates that limit
instructors' creativity and freedom. They become discouraged by
their own limitations in making meaningful change. Every year, up
to six percent of the nation's teachers leave the profession." She also
warns of the consequences of ignoring the plight of teachers, particularly in urban schools: "Study after study has shown that a stable,
long-term faculty is a key determinant in student achievement.
Constant turnover robs schools of the cohesion and sense of community critical to their success."

How to Lead by Standing Behind

Based on the reports of our teachers, it appears that effective trans-formational principals are quite creative and aggressive in standing behind their teachers. Principals support their schools' instructional goals by serving as resource providers and guardians of instructional time. They assist teachers with student discipline matters, allow teachers to develop discipline codes, and support teachers' authority in enforcing policy. Even when teachers err, they are allowed to "save face" before parents and students. Also in recognition of teach-ers' professionalism, effective principals are creative in making the workplace more attractive to teachers by sponsoring special events in their honor. The following lessons are gleaned from the many forms of support noted by the teachers in our study.

1. Devote ample time to orient new teachers to school and district resources, including print and film media, equipment, textbooks, and supplies.

   Explain policies for use of equipment and encourage teachers to seek assistance when needed. If supplies are rationed, explain the rationale as well as the policy. Remember that the novice has not had time to build a personal library of resources; provide access to catalogs and funds for the purchase of supplemental materials.

2. Ensure that all teachers have a sufficient number of appropriate textbooks and materials for all students.

   Check resources before school begins and periodically solicit input from teachers regarding appropriateness and adequacy. Do not make demands that teachers cannot meet because of limited resources.

3. Provide the means for teachers to attend professional development conferences.

   Whenever possible, registration fees for conferences should be paid for teachers, and substitutes should be provided to cover classes missed. Astute principals keep informed of professional development opportunities for teachers and encourage participation. All reasonable requests for teachers to attend conferences and seminars should be entertained.

4. Collaborate with teachers to write school improvement grants.

   Rather than lament the inadequacy of funds necessary to produce meaningful educational change, aggressive principals seek alternative sources of funding from business partnerships and federal, state, and local grants.

5. Work with teachers to develop and implement a student discipline policy.

   Ensure that a clearly written policy exists for addressing problems of student conduct. When violations occur, enforce the policy consistently and in a timely manner.

6. Support teachers' decisions on discipline issues unless those decisions are inconsistent with written policy.

   In spite of formalized procedures, some cases will require subjective judgment. Unless the teacher's decision is inconsistent with written policy or unfair to the student, support the teacher's authority. If it becomes necessary to rule against the teacher, carefully explain the decision in private.

7. Monitor and develop teachers' classroom management skills.

   Many teachers leave the profession in the early years because they never learn to manage student discipline. Assure that every teacher has a reasonable opportunity to develop proficiency in instruction by providing assistance in classroom management.

8. Take time to listen to teachers who have problems with student discipline.

   In many cases, empathy is all that teachers need to resolve their own student discipline problems. Give them the time to voice their concerns, listening carefully for signs that corrective measures are warranted and offering assistance if desired.

9. Limit the number of scheduled meetings.

Effective principals covet planning and instructional time. Whole faculty meetings are kept to a minimum. Memos and small group meetings often serve the same needs.

10. Limit paperwork.

Teacher aides and secretarial staff should be used to limit the amount of teacher time required for paperwork. To the extent possible, reporting functions should be centralized.

11. Provide creative tangible rewards.

In a much-criticized and underpaid profession, small rewards greatly improve morale. Seize every opportunity to brighten teachers' work lives with visible signs of appreciation, such as small gifts, release time, or periodic refreshments.

CHAPTER SEVEN

Gentle Nudges

Suggesting Versus Directing

> *Our principal was able to influence us to develop our curriculum thoroughly. Through the force of his leadership, we generated course goals and behavioral objectives, carefully linked them to an articulated curriculum, and developed an integrated scope and sequence for our content area in Grades 7 through 9. This was a new area for all of us at the time and it was not something we did willingly. [He] didn't force us to do this work. He carefully, logically, and gently laid out the research on the importance of this kind of curriculum development and then paid us to write it. He was flexible about the hours we worked and the amount of time we spent at lunch. He would stop by as we worked, always seeming interested in our work—not checking up on us.*

> —A middle school teacher

Several of the strategies discussed in earlier chapters, such as praise and rewards, are used by effective principals to improve teacher morale. Others, such as involvement and expectations, are used to improve teacher commitment. Some, such as providing adequate resources, ensure that teachers are able to perform effectively.

Many of the strategies discussed thus far indirectly affect classroom instruction. Teachers who are more involved in schoolwide decisions, for example, report being more innovative; those whose

80

efforts are acknowledged report being revitalized. Other strategies, however, are intended to improve instruction more directly.

Because administrative authority in the realm of instruction is limited by teachers' desires for professionalism and autonomy, strategies used by principals to improve instruction must be used with considerable diplomacy. Principals must demonstrate respect for teachers' choices and acceptance of multiple teaching styles and strategies. Their help must be perceived by teachers not as orders, but as friendly, concerned advice. For this reason, we refer to this group of strategies as "gentle nudges." Similarly, Allen, Glickman, and Hensley (1998) found that 66 percent of the principals they studied had come to view their role as that of encourager, supporter, or enabler. Gurr, Drysdale, and Mulford (2006) studied successful school leaders in Tasmania and Victoria, Australia. They referred to these leaders as other-centered and empathic, but with the resolve to ensure student learning through open and honest communication with teachers. Such gentle nudges took several forms in our study; the most frequent were related to providing teachers with professional literature, training opportunities, and suggestions.

APPROPRIATE INTERVENTION

Although effective transformational principals typically use indirect methods of intervention, such as advice, in some cases they simply tell teachers what to do or act on teachers' behalf. These occasions include crisis situations and requests for help.

We found that principals use direct intervention primarily in response to teacher requests. When their help was requested, the principals described by teachers in our study were likely to intercede quickly and report back to the teacher initiating the request.

The principal's assistance with a range of problems—instructional and noninstructional in nature—was solicited by teachers in the study. For example, a female teacher reported being sexually harassed by another teacher. When notified, her principal immediately took control of the situation: "She listened . . . told me exactly what she was going to do . . . and asked me later if there was still a problem." In addition to resolution of the immediate problem, increased teacher respect for the principal was a direct outcome of this encounter. The teacher was relieved and appreciative that "[the principal] did not treat me as though I was crazy or as though I asked for it."

In crisis situations, effective principals also use direct intervention to affect teachers' performance. In these cases, the urgency of the situation requires that the principal give orders rather than suggest strategies. Principals use directives to prevent further escalation of crises. They explain situations to their teachers, anticipate possible consequences, and give specific directions for dealing with those consequences.

Principals who use direct intervention in crises are successful in limiting loss and containing disorder. Teachers expressed relief at being told how to act under stressful circumstances:

> When a student committed suicide [the principal] held a
> morning faculty meeting in which he communicated all the
> information we needed . . . how to address students . . . "what if"
> types of situations we might be confronted with. . . . I was able to
> comfort, answer questions, send the students who needed special
> help to the appropriate source, and handle the situation
> professionally.

HAVE YOU CONSIDERED. . . . ?

Under more typical circumstances, effective principals use fewer directives; instead, they influence teachers through advice or suggestion. Effective principals studied by Blumberg (1989) were quite candid about their use of suggestion. Understanding that curriculum and instruction were the "territorial prerogatives" (p. 144) of teachers, these principals planted suggestions for consideration rather than intruding into teachers' domain. Blumberg refers to this technique as "seeding." Principals consider all possible alternatives to an instructional problem and select those that are acceptable, then present only those to teachers. Thus, they inform teachers of the alternatives they prefer, but soften their involvement by allowing teachers to control final choices about matters in their professional realm. In a recent study of teachers, Blase and Blase (2004) confirm the importance of suggestions in influencing and motivating classroom behavior.

Knuth (2006) and Marzano, Waters, and McNulty (2005) proposed the use of the "Monday Memo" to communicate with teachers. Knuth uses what he terms Level One and Level Two Communications. Level One Communications are routine but necessary and effectively conveyed through written memos. Level Two Communications are more personalized. They are intended to build relationships and convey the principal's vision and expectations. Monday Memos are one mechanism for communicating Level One and Level Two expectations to teachers.

Teachers in our study also reported that transformational principals motivate them to examine alternative instructional methods by relying on interpersonal diplomacy and informal conversation. When teachers ask for help with an instructional matter or when a problem is perceived by the principal, these principals present options for teacher consideration. Rather than require teachers to correct their deficits in a prescribed manner, principals allow teachers to make choices from among alternatives. As one teacher reported:

> *[My principal] will ask for my opinion on how to do things and then offer suggestions. . . . He may ask if I considered trying a particular way of doing a task. . . . I tend to be open to his suggestions and willing to give consideration to his ideas.*

As a result, some teachers disclosed that they became more reflective about their own decisions. Some responded selectively to their principals' suggestions. As one teacher noted, "I have begun to use some ideas in formulating my own theories rather than accept something she says." In most cases, teachers reported accepting or trying some aspect of the principal's advice.

The language used by principals to offer ideas for improvement reflects the fragile, tenuous nature of the authority relationship between principal and teacher in the area of curriculum and instruction. Principals deemphasize their power by suggesting rather than directing, but further deemphasis is noted in the presentation of suggestions. Principals usually do not portend to know the best course of action. Instead, they present advice through questions, such as "Have you considered . . . ?" or "What if you tried . . . ?" One principal was described as follows:

> *[He's] not the type to directly tell you to do something. This is very good because it creates a positive atmosphere. . . . He believes his teachers should have input on every area of our school. . . . When we discuss discipline, he uses questioning as a means of influence . . . a question such as "Don't you think . . . ?"*

In response to this indirect and nonthreatening mode of instructional supervision, teachers reported feeling "relieved," "relaxed," and "free." Professional autonomy is a direct outcome: "I am given the benefit of making the decision on my own." Direct effects on performance were noted in nearly every case:

- "I will give things a try because I do not feel threatened if they fail."
- "I try to conform to what I feel she wants."
- "I try to do a better job . . . work harder to make a unit more successful."

POWER IN EMPOWERING

Faculty empowerment is often narrowly construed as participation in decision making. Maeroff (1988), an early empowerment theorist, argues that empowerment requires elevating teachers in terms of status and knowledge as well as giving them access to school-wide decision making. He views staff development as an appropriate vehicle for increasing teacher status and knowledge. Recent works of others strongly support Maeroff's argument (Blase & Blase, 2004; Clift, Johnson, Holland, & Veal, 1992; Johnson, 2006; Short & Rinehart, 1992).

Administrators are realizing more and more that empowering teachers requires more than providing opportunities to act to achieve school goals. Decision participation alone may not increase teachers' power to improve schools. Of equal importance (and perhaps this is a prerequisite) is helping to develop the ability to act, which is achieved through enhancement of teachers' knowledge. Teachers must be provided opportunities to acquire the knowledge necessary to warrant classroom autonomy and authority over schoolwide decisions (Kirby, 1992). As Hawley (1988) cautions, the ability of restructured schools (of which faculty empowerment is a critical component) to improve student achievement is "conditioned by the collective competence levels of the teachers involved" (p. 427). Johnson (2006) further notes that opportunities to develop competence through professional development are brokered by the principal.

Our study indicates that effective principals do not accept teacher skill and knowledge as bounded by past learning. In addition to suggesting techniques for instructional improvement, effective principals use two other subtle strategies to increase teachers' knowledge: They create opportunities for professional development and they provide teachers with current professional literature.

Professional Development

Principals provided teachers in our study with both formal and informal opportunities to develop practical knowledge and skills. Informally, the principals made themselves available to assist teachers as needed. They often provided assistance in areas of special interest; several principals, for example, assisted teachers with computer use for instructional and record-keeping purposes.

Among the other topics of particular interest to the principals were drug use, divorce, death, and child abuse. Formal training sessions, often conducted by outside experts, provided teachers with information about these topics. Staff development in curriculum and in instruction issues, such as language methods and questioning strategies, also was provided.

Perhaps as important as the specific topics chosen for staff development is the discretion afforded teachers in selecting which components to implement and which to ignore. The teachers felt that they

could reflect on newly acquired information and choose those pieces
most beneficial to them and their students:

> *The principal is a big advocate of whole language instruction,*
> *and, as a school goal last year, did whatever she could to make*
> *sure the implementation of the program flowed smoothly.*
> *Teachers were trained throughout the previous year. They were*
> *not mandated to implement the program, but were encouraged*
> *to implement the parts that they were comfortable with. I guess*
> *she trusted us and let us go at it! I felt so comfortable in the*
> *school, implementing parts of the program. I had the freedom to*
> *be creative, and my children benefited most.*

The behavioral and affective outcomes that the teachers associate with training are quite positive. They reported feeling "confident" and "appreciative." Their awareness of important issues—such
as the role of expectations in student performance or the process and
purpose of empowerment—increased. Changes in teacher behavior
were generally consistent with the purposes of training. For example,
computer training sessions tended to increase teachers' use of com-
puters in the classroom. New discipline and instructional techniques
were practiced, albeit with some selectivity.

Two factors explain the effectiveness of this strategy in affecting
teacher performance. As mentioned earlier, discretion in implementing new learning allows teachers to retain control over decisions
affecting their classrooms. Additionally, pragmatism is used to
explain the effectiveness of training. For many teachers, knowing
that "the children benefit from it . . . makes it worthwhile."

Professional Literature

A final strategy used by effective transformational principals to
influence instruction is providing teachers with professional literature. Unfortunately, many educators tend to limit their search for
assistance to other teachers in the same building. This may further
compound the isolation that characterizes teaching and also may
restrict opportunities for creative and current improvement options.
But researchers have learned that principals in highly collaborative

professional cultures encourage many forms of staff development, including training and dissemination of professional literature (Leithwood, 1994; Leithwood & Jantzi, 2000). Effective staff development acknowledges that one's own colleagues, as well as external experts, possess useful information for guiding school improvement efforts. Effective staff development fosters collaboration, which in turn fosters a desire for further growth. Thus, the principal who promotes faculty growth and involvement will provide ample resources and opportunities for development.

The effective principals discussed by teachers in our study kept abreast of trends in instruction and curriculum, informed teachers of these advancements, and encouraged them to try new techniques. By doing so, they were able to expand teachers' abilities to improve instruction and to support their belief that improvement is possible with attention to empirical evidence documented by others.

Teachers also explained that effective principals distribute articles from research and professional journals, magazines, and newspapers. In most cases, these are related to effective teaching or effective schools' practices. Curriculum writing, discipline techniques, and computer use also are covered, but less frequently. In essence, their principals use the gentle nudging approach, placing literature in teachers' mailboxes with little or no further comment:

> *The principal of our school is interested in improvement of instruction which he verbalizes in faculty meetings and in informal school settings. He relates research and theories in small-talk situations. He also places in our mailboxes little thought-provoking ideas concerning teaching effectiveness. . . . People tend to read and discuss much of the effectiveness tidbits.*

Some principals are very explicit about their expectations for the use of professional literature. One principal told teachers that they were to read the materials and then provided time for them to discuss the content. During this time they were also to plan how they would apply the information. Other principals were less directive.

From the teachers' perspective, dissemination of professional literature enhances their awareness and motivation to improve.

Consider these pragmatic and open-minded attitudes expressed by teachers:

- "I feel like I'm at least somewhat current on key issues in education . . . I reassess my attitudes after reading the articles."
- "It makes me more interested in various educational strategies and motivates me to improve on my own . . . I can try if I want."

The latter comment emphasizes again the importance of allowing teachers choice about whether or not to implement the strategies they have read about. This may account for the very positive attitude the majority of teachers took toward this influence strategy.

One more skeptical teacher noted that "it would take a lot more time, money, and effort to dramatically change teachers' methods of doing things after they have been ingrained over several years." As Leithwood and his associates note (Leithwood, 1994; Leithwood & Jantzi, 2000; Leithwood et al., 1996a), teachers are much more open to growth opportunities such as professional literature when a strong commitment to school improvement goals exists. The interactive nature of professional development, goal commitment, and work collaboration deserves considerable attention by those attempting to influence teacher growth. The reader should keep in mind that none of these strategies is used in isolation. Furthermore, although teachers rate each strategy as highly effective in influencing their performance, they judge their principals in general to be effective on the basis of their overall approach, not on the basis of any one strategy. Effective principals who work to enhance professional growth undoubtedly also build faculty involvement.

A second caution is also in order regarding the use of professional literature. Overall teaching is positively influenced by this strategy. Some teachers try new instructional techniques: "I try more ideas and techniques . . . I believe I have increased my effectiveness." Classroom demeanor is affected as well. A teacher who had been given some literature on the effects of teacher attitude toward students remarked, "I changed my actions. For example, this fall I made an effort to be gracious in welcoming new students to my already overcrowded classroom." Our data suggest that long-lasting effects of the use of professional literature are not guaranteed, however. A teacher describing what occurred in her school commented that "most teachers, including myself, used the methods for a while and then got bogged down with the details." This suggests a need to follow dissemination of materials with encouragement and monitoring regarding implementation as well as follow-up help, if needed.

Overall, teachers rated the use of professional literature as quite effective in influencing their classroom behavior. Their explanations for effectiveness shed some light on how the strategy can best be used. First, principals were careful not to overload teachers with complex or abundant materials. One teacher commented that "the ideas are simple teaching or management ideas that can be easily incorporated into lessons. Given just one idea now and then it's not overwhelming and more apt to be tried." A second justification was the emphasis on teacher discretion, which was equated with professional respect: "[The principal] gave us freedom as we worked. He valued us as professionals." Finally, respect for the principal made this an acceptable strategy for many teachers: "I have great respect for her . . . and feel that her judgments are worth my efforts."

ON NUDGING AND INTRUDING

Our data suggest that effective principals know when it is appropriate to intrude into teachers' workspaces and when it is advantageous to tread more cautiously. During crisis situations, when immediate action is necessary to prevent further damage, or when asked for help, these principals act quickly and decisively.

In the realm of instruction, principals' personal desires to intervene, even where they see opportunities for improvement, are tempered by their respect for teachers' knowledge and appreciation for their feelings. On instructional matters, therefore, they advise, suggest, provide information, and create opportunities for advanced training. Seldom do they issue directives. This softened entry into teachers' "territory" is accepted and quite effective in influencing changes in teacher behavior. With regard to the strategies we refer to collectively as gentle nudging, we offer the following recommendations for principals' consideration.

1. Know when to push and when to nudge.

   Effective principals do not hesitate to give specific direct instructions during crises. Also, when teachers request their help, they show genuine concern and take deliberate steps to help resolve the problem.

2. Know how to give advice, particularly regarding instruction.

   Rather than force teachers to comply with one preferred method, effective principals provide teachers with several acceptable alternatives. Further, they provide advice as offers of help from one colleague to another. The language of suggestion often takes the form of questions.

3. Provide training opportunities to reinforce goals and improve instruction.

   Effective principals assume that all teachers have room for professional growth. They share their own expertise with teachers, provide teachers opportunities to learn from one another, and invite external experts to assist in staff development.

4. Allow discretion in implementation of knowledge gained through staff development.

   Perhaps one of the most essential requirements of successful training is the opportunity for teachers to evaluate the efficacy of changing their methods and then respecting their ultimate judgments.

5. Assist teachers in evaluating newly attempted techniques.

   New methods may be dropped by teachers because they initially require more time and effort. Efforts must be acknowledged and encouraged, and assistance should be provided in assessing the relative merit of the new approach.

6. Keep informed of new developments in curriculum and instruction and provide relevant information to teachers.

To have credibility as instructional leaders, principals must take the time to keep current on trends in curriculum and instruction. They can help teachers remain current and improve their skills if they sort, select, and disseminate professional materials of relevance to classroom and school performance. Materials should be limited to those that are relevant to a specific teacher's needs or to schoolwide goals. They should not be difficult to interpret and should provide meaningful, concrete suggestions for teacher use.

CHAPTER EIGHT

Positive Use of Formal Authority

> *I have an authoritative principal, one who is warm but firm. Her excellent reputation and track record have proven that she makes wise decisions. Therefore, when she speaks, teachers listen and do. She transmits her requests to the faculty through meetings and newsletters. If the request is not carried out properly, she will reprimand that teacher privately. If it is carried out properly, she will sing your praises. She directly lets the faculty know at all times what she expects.*
>
> *Nothing slips by my principal. She keeps me on my toes. Her goal is to provide a positive learning environment for the students. Nothing will stand in her way of accomplishing it. This has a positive effect on me. It makes me want to please her more by giving 110%.*
>
> —An elementary school teacher

Formal authority is derived from the position held in a bureau-cratic hierarchy. When asked to recollect influence strategies used by their principals, few teachers in our study volunteered that they comply out of respect for the principal's position alone. In fact, teachers and principals alike often view an over-reliance on formal authority by administrators as degrading and condescending. They resent being expected to suppress their intellect and creativity. According to Argyris (1957), workers are often expected to concede to formal authority because supervisors assume that workers, like infants, are incapable of self-direction and self-discipline. Similarly, McGregor (1960) has argued that administrators who hold Theory X assumptions about workers (i.e., that they dislike work, lack initiative, and resist change) tend to be directive and authoritarian leaders. It is important to remember that formal authority is limited in scope in educational organizations (Blase & Blase, 2001; Hoy & Miskel, 2005) and as Weber (1947) argued early on, people tend to obey authority they see as legitimate; that is, authority is based on voluntary compliance. Moreover, Heifetz (1998) noted that authority can actually impede leadership because it promotes "inappropriate dependencies" and may delude those in authority into thinking that only they can make good decisions.

Dependence on formal authority alone flounders in the new era of educational reform for school improvement. Instead, collaboration, empowerment, and shared leadership are heralded by many as the only enduring means for reversing the failure of schooling in America (e.g., Glickman, 1993; Leithwood & Jantzi, 2000; Murphy & Datnow, 2003; Murphy & Louis, 1994; Waters, Marzano & McNulty, 2003). With teachers demanding a voice in school governance, any hint of autocracy raises the battle cry. Power is vested not in rank or title, but in those with valued expertise and strong interpersonal skills. Power and influence are functions of the person, not only the position.

Hersey, Blanchard, and Natemeyer (1976) developed a model describing seven bases of power. Bases of power determined by one's position include the power to dispense rewards, the power to sanction or punish, the power of the office (e.g., exercised through evaluation, hiring, and firing),[1] and the power based on knowing influential people. Three bases reside in the person: the power of expertise, the power of information, and the power of personality. Teacher satisfaction is negatively associated with overuse of position power. Clearly a positive relation exists between the use of personal power by administrators and higher levels of teacher professionalism. In part, the preference for personal power may be a function of sex-role stereotyping due to the large number of females in administrative positions in schools. Several research studies have confirmed that followers prefer that women leaders demonstrate strong consideration (e.g., kindness, thoughtfulness, respect) for followers. Although consideration also is viewed as an important leader behavior for males, it is frequently central to the leadership of female principals and has considerable influence with teachers (Beck, 1994; Noddings, 1992; Sergiovanni, 1992; Shakeshaft, 1987).

The type of organization—static or dynamic—may further influence preferences for a particular leadership style. In dynamic school organizations, power is dispersed, individual initiative is valued, and decision making is shared (Owens & Valesky, 2007; Sergiovanni, 2001). In such organizations, because there is a deemphasis on hierarchy and formal authority—realms in which males traditionally are perceived as more effective—women may be expected to emerge as leaders (Dunlap & Schmuck, 1995; Noddings, 1992; Women's Educational Equity Act Publishing Center, 1990). Problems associated with position power in education, then, may be a function of both the increasing professionalization of teaching, which transforms schools into more dynamic organizations, and sex-role stereotyping, which limits the options available to female principals for successfully influencing teachers.

EFFECTIVE USE OF FORMAL AUTHORITY

Although the research on sex-role expectations is limited and inconclusive, there is considerable evidence that people prefer a democratic style of leadership from leaders of either sex. Hersey et al. (1976) contend that more mature (i.e., experienced, willing, competent) followers are less influenced by the use of position power. The effect of formal authority, therefore, is attenuated by the re-culturing of schools where teachers are viewed as professionals (i.e., mature professionals) and where shared decision making for school improvement is valued. Hersey, Blanchard, and Johnson (1996) point out that administrators should modify their approach to leadership to accommodate such changes.

Given this devaluing of formal authority, it is not surprising that the teachers in our study qualified their responses to its influence. They reported that transformational principals do use the authority of their office to influence teacher behavior, but teachers noted in all cases that principals do so equitably and respectfully. In several cases, teachers rationalized that principals need to rely on the power of their position to influence less competent teachers. This is consistent with Hersey et al.'s (1976) situational leadership theory—less mature followers (in this case, less competent teachers) respond more readily to use of position power. This is also important because the use of formal authority will tend to negate forms of personal power that are more effective (Hoy & Miskel, 2005).

Our teachers also reported that principals use authority to uphold district policies and reinforce fundamental norms such as fairness and maximum use of allocated learning time. Frequently reported instructional goals are related to student rights and needs:

> *She has always insisted that what is done for one class must be done for all 10 classes. It was very hard for me to begin to think of not just my class of first graders and what they need and what I can do for them. After five years, I have seen the results of caring that every child in the first grade learn to read and not just my class of 25. It has made me more aware of all children in my grade level and has helped me help new teachers so that their classes could achieve as well as mine.*

Effective principals insist that all students have equal exposure to content and that they be tested fairly. They told the teachers in our study to ensure "bell-to-bell teaching" and early involvement from parents. Punctuality, compliance with state standards and district policies, and awareness of duties and responsibilities are among the noninstructional goals associated with the use of authority.

Accepted Uses of Authority

Although the use of formal authority in schools is very limited in scope (Hoy & Miskel, 2005), according to teachers, principals exercise authority when they assign specific duties to teachers or appoint teachers to committees. They use authority when they develop a new instructional objective or school policy. They use authority when they enforce rules or mandate action. In contrast to most other strategies reported by teachers, authority is viewed as quite direct. As the terms associated with its use imply, it is exercised unilaterally; when used, little negotiation or bargaining is evident.

How then are some principals able to use authority effectively without appearing to be forceful or insensitive? Apparently, the use of authority is accepted because teachers believe it is used fairly to achieve positive outcomes for others—not as a manipulative tactic for the principal's personal gain. It is also used in the context of a positive professional relationship with teachers based on the principal's wise reliance on personal power. The following excerpts from teachers' responses demonstrate this nonmanipulative, humanitarian use of authority:

- "He requires teachers to communicate in a positive manner with students."
- "He assigns work to everyone equally."
- "My principal does not want us to allow students to fail because they refuse to turn in work. We must talk to them, contact parents, and send students to the office if they do not do their work. Only after we have exhausted all methods can we give them a zero."
- "He required that we write a positive letter for each six-week grading period to parents for a student that we felt deserved recognition."

At times, principals use authority to make final decisions after soliciting input from teachers: "He explains what needs to be done, answers questions that anyone might have, evaluates suggestions, and selects a course of action." This limited "consultative" approach is accepted by some teachers because decisions are perceived to be based on school need and an awareness of teachers' problems. As one teacher commented, her principal made most decisions, but only after "listening to the flow of the school." Often teachers accept their principals' authority because of the principal's history of making competent and consistent decisions:

> *[My principal] is firm but fair with the way that she deals with faculty and students. When teachers don't follow the rules, she calls them into her office and informs them that they will follow the rules or she will find someone who can. I feel secure in the knowledge that the rules are in place for everyone without regard to area taught, [whether one is a] coach or noncoach, etc.*

The exercise of authority had mixed effects on the feelings and behaviors of teachers in our study. Approximately 60 percent of the feelings associated with authority were positive. Teachers used "comfortable," "secure," and "encouraged" to describe their reactions to this form of influence. Several teachers reported initially having negative reactions to the use of authority, but their feelings changed when they understood the principals' rationale for its use. For example, one teacher was upset that teachers had not been involved in pre-planning, but she accepted the principal's plan because it was educationally sound. She rationalized that "if just one student learns, it will be worth it."

Behaviorally, most teachers comply with the wishes of principals who use authority. Specific effects include more positive attitudes toward students, increased contact with parents, and adherence to rules and deadlines. Not surprisingly, Leithwood and Jantzi (2000) found that use of contingent rewards—the ability to dispense rewards based on position of authority—is often related to transformational leadership behaviors that have positive effects on teachers and students.

NEGATIVE EFFECTS

In the introduction to this chapter, we discuss the problems related to the use of formal authority. It should not be inferred from our data that these obstacles are entirely overcome by transformational principals simply because they recognize appropriate uses of authority. Quite the contrary: Of the teachers who reported authority as one means of influence used by their principals, 40 percent identified negative outcomes connected with its use. They noted feelings of anger, resentment, guilt, rebelliousness, depression, intimidation, and manipulation.

The remarks of some teachers reveal that they equate the use of authority with their principals' assumptions that teachers are immature—incapable of setting their own priorities, managing time, or assuming responsibility. Very often, teachers explained, these principals implement and enforce rules to monitor teacher behavior.

Sign-in sheets were mentioned by several teachers as an ongoing source of frustration. One teacher noted how monitoring of punctuality could be used to induce feelings of guilt and humiliation: "[The principal] takes up the sign-in sheet when people come in late. This makes you be on time or you must go see her to sign in."

Planning is another area of teachers' lives monitored by principals. Teachers often are required to turn in weekly lesson plans. Although the practice may be district mandated, some teachers view its strict implementation as an unnecessary display of authority by the principal:

> I resent the use of time to write specific lesson plans that I feel could be used in a more productive way. I do it because I have to, just like I did in college. But at times I get angry because I need that time to have parent conferences, work on student lessons, meet with individual students to discuss goals.

In addition, principals monitor teachers' grading practices. Some require that teachers submit copies of their grading policies each year. Others reserve the right to preview report card grades before the cards are sent home to parents. The most resented practice, however, is an order from the principal to change a student's grade. Some teachers eventually compromise their standards to avoid confrontation: "I am more hesitant in sending home failing grades and unsatisfactory conduct grades." When confronted, others buckle to authority by principals: "We do what we are assigned. . . . You get in trouble if you buck the system"; "When you don't, you get reprimanded as a child would." Although teachers comply with their principals' directives, principals' self-appointed veto power over student grades has bitter repercussions:

> *I am angry and frustrated. I was disappointed in myself for not refusing to change the grade the child earned . . . It's unfair to give a false picture of a child's academic success. I do not feel that it was ethical for an administrator to disregard the evaluation of a child.*

Moreover, misuse of formal authority with one teacher can have a "ripple effect" throughout the school, causing those who hear about or witness its misuse to lose respect for and distrust the principal. A teacher's complaint about an injustice resulting from the misuse of authority will likely produce undesirable effects on others in the school (Porter, Bigley, & Steers, 2003).

THE SELECTIVE USE OF AUTHORITY

The reader may now be left with a mixed message with regard to the use of authority. Although it is frequently reported as an effective influence strategy, its use often leaves teachers feeling resentful. Teachers seem to accept that there are some appropriate times to draw on legitimate power, but they seldom feel that the time is appropriate for them. Thus, authority must be invoked with extreme care. It should not be used to perpetuate humiliating rules, nor should it be used without justification. With these caveats in mind, we offer the following suggestions for the selective use of authority.

1. Work to change bureaucratic rules and policies that reduce teachers' status.

We do not advocate anarchy, but we do recognize that principals create rules for control of the few who are not self-managing. A professional (adult) view of teachers requires that conditions that cast them as children be eliminated. Peters (1987) advises managers to eliminate bureaucratic rules and humiliating conditions. Sign-in sheets, overly detailed lesson plans, and close scrutiny of teacher-assigned grades are three practices that teachers find demeaning. Consider eliminating them. If such rules are mandated by the school district, work to get them changed. When policies are violated, monitor only the violator.

2. Where authority is necessary to enforce necessary rules or policies, justify its use in ethical terms.

Keep in mind that effective principals used authority to influence teachers in our study, and that 60 percent of the teachers reported no negative feelings associated with this strategy. Many rationalized its use because it was equitable to teachers and in the best interest of students. Student grades, for example, should be objectively defensible. Principals may wish to review teachers' grading practices or assigned grades to guarantee fair treatment of students. They may insist that teachers exercise all available means of assistance before failing students. These uses of authority will be tolerated more easily by teachers if the humanitarian treatment of students is always the stated purpose.

3. Solicit input in creating policies that may have to be enforced through the exercise of authority.

Teachers are less resentful over the use of authority to enforce decisions that are made collectively. Granting teachers a voice in school decisions serves two purposes here: It is based on a professional view of teachers that buffers the negative effect of formal authority, and it creates ownership for the decision. Thus, if monitoring or enforcement through authority becomes necessary, teachers are likely to be more supportive. To resolve the lesson plan dilemma, for example, teachers might be asked to create a method for ensuring that all teachers are prepared for their classes, but one that is more than a perfunctory exercise in documentation. They may develop a plan for verbal checks, simplified written plans, or peer monitoring. If given the freedom to develop their own policies, teachers are likely to become self-policing.

4. Accept that there are appropriate times to exercise authority.

   Research on sex-role stereotyping suggests that followers may expect less authoritative behavior from females, but this research is far from conclusive. Principals might look to situational leadership theories for guidance rather than comply with role expectations. Situational theorists suggest that the use of authority should be determined by the maturity of teachers; that is, their willingness and ability to perform as expected in relation to the demands of a given task. Teachers who are less competent or less experienced require more directive guidance and closer monitoring. As an example, teachers whose daily lesson plans have been impeccable for the first three months of the school year might be allowed to turn in monthly summary plans for the remainder of the year. Of course, any practice that may be construed as unequal treatment of teachers must be objective, and the basis for differential treatment (e.g., records of poor lesson plans or number of times teacher arrived late) must be documented.

5. Dispense authoritative punishments with care.

   At times, it is necessary for principals to use their authority to discipline teachers. Such authority should be used sparingly and only for legitimate purposes; its misuse can have seriously deleterious effects on teachers in general and on a principal's positive relationships with teachers. Yukl's (2006) guidelines for the proper use of authority surely will help ameliorate many potentially negative effects of using one's formal authority to discipline teachers: explain rules and requirements, respond to problems frankly and fairly,

collect the facts prior to dispensing discipline, give warnings
when appropriate and do so privately, remain calm, do
not exhibit hostility, indicate a willingness to help, solicit
feedback from the individual about the problem and ways to
improve, and use only punishments that correspond to the
seriousness of the problem.

NOTE

1. It is interesting to note that French and Raven (1968), and
   later Hersey, Blanchard, and Natemeyer (1976), refer to
   the power of office as *legitimate* power. They use the term
   in a legalistic sense. If *legitimate* is used to mean valid or
   acceptable, then the most legitimate power from a teacher's
   perspective is personal power.

CHAPTER NINE

Mirrors to the Possible

*Our principal is supportive and personally concerned with his
teachers' professional careers and outside interests. He is
involved with students' extracurricular activities such as Special
Olympics. He takes an interest in classroom activities and takes
time to visit classrooms informally. He brags to visitors about
his teachers and their programs. He has a positive attitude about
his job, which encourages a good attitude [among others]. He is
very concerned with keeping an upbeat attitude in a school
situation that tends to be depressing and discouraging. It works.
Teachers in the school are as concerned and involved with the
principal as he is with us.*

—An elementary school teacher

To this point, we have discussed strategies of effective transformational school principals that teachers in our study recognize
as particularly powerful in influencing their behavior. But the teachers also commented extensively on the personality of leaders. They
identified certain aspects of their principals' personality and
demeanor that contributed to principals' effectiveness as leaders. In
particular, the teachers found that effective principals are highly visible and model attitudes and behaviors consistent with personal values and with the expectations they hold for teachers. Teachers see
these principals as expressing changes in schooling that are both
desirable and possible.

Personality has long been recognized as an important dimension of leader effectiveness. Some people are more inspiring, more likable, more appealing than others. These persons frequently emerge as leaders. *Referent power* is the term used to refer to one's ability to influence based on personality. In the extreme form, it is called charisma.

Max Weber borrowed the concept of charisma from theology, where it was considered to be a gift bestowed by God. For Weber, charisma is a mystical, magnetic attraction that some individuals acquire in times of crisis. Others follow the charismatic, believing that they too will be connected to transcendent powers by virtue of association with the charismatic (Bass, 1988).

The definition of charisma has evolved since Weber's conceptualization, but not without controversy. Many theorists no longer believe that charismatic leadership emerges only in situations of crisis, for example. But the exact qualifications of the charismatic are no less clear today than they were when charisma was believed to be a gift from God. According to Bass (1988), two essential elements of the charismatic relationship are a strong desire by followers to identify with the leader, and the leader's possession of certain abilities, traits, and interests. Among the latter, Bass includes emotional expressiveness or dramatic flair, self-confidence, conviction in one's beliefs, eloquence, insight, and high levels of energy. Using this definition of charisma as dramatic flair, Lawler (1984), for example, argued that more educated followers are less influenced by charisma than the less educated.

More recently, Leithwood, Louis, Anderson, and Wahlstrom (2004b) identified what they term a "developing people" dimension of school leadership which is much like Burns's (1978) original definition of charisma which had a distinct moral dimension and was less tied to rhetorical technique. According to Burns, leaders serve as role models for others as they demonstrate their conviction to a clear set of values. Unlike Bass, Leithwood and Jantzi (2000) dropped the term "charisma" from their description of transformational leaders. Rather than describing personality traits, they prefer to describe those leader behaviors that change (i.e., transform) organizations for the better.

Rather than ask whether the effective principals described in our study are charismatic, we ask whether they are transformational. According to teachers, aspects of principals' personality that are most influential are their honesty, optimism, and consideration. Further, principals are able to (and do) model the behaviors they expect from teachers, and they are highly visible in their schools. Although the principals described to us are certainly liked and respected by their teachers, they are not simply depicted as dramatic, highly inspirational, and magnetic; in fact, few are described in terms typically associated with Bass's definition of charisma, yet they are similar to the transformational leaders described by Leithwood and Jantzi (2000) and earlier by Burns (1978). The responses of teachers in our study are consistent with Kouzes and Posner's (1990) and Graseck's (2005) findings: effective principals are repeatedly described as honest. They maintain very positive attitudes and sincere beliefs that they and their teachers will improve education for students. They demonstrate their own competence by modeling the skills and behaviors they expect from teachers. Teachers added that effective principals show consideration, another behavior described by Leithwood and Jantzi as transformational.

Leadership based on the values of honesty, optimism, and consideration differs in fundamental ways from leadership based on Bass's popular definition of charisma. Most notable among the differences is that the former is grounded in morality, whereas the latter is grounded in personality. Moral leaders incorporate an ethic of caring into a vision of what is best and possible for all students (Beck & Murphy, 1994; Bolman & Deal, 1995; Marshall, Patterson, Rogers, & Steele, 1996; Murphy, 2006; Noddings, 1992). In achieving their vision, they ask no more of others than they expect from themselves. Their actions and words are consistent, and they are genuine in their interactions with others.

Numerous scholars have raised questions about the field of educational administration's preoccupation with bureaucracy and failure to recognize the place of values in discourse (Beck & Murphy, 1994; Blase & Anderson, 1995; Dempster, Freakley, & Parry, 2001; Evers & Lakomski, 1993; Hodgkinson, 1991; Willower, 1994). William Foster (1991, p. 20) criticizes the field of educational administration for its "bureaucratic concern with efficiency" and banning of values from discourse. In the scientific-positivist tradition that has dominated educational administration, he argues, decisions are evaluated on the basis of rules and procedures, rather than on the basis of what is moral or right. Education can no more be amoral than can it be apolitical, however. Foster argues that administrators could help transform schooling through open critique, caring, and inclusion. Administrators who are able to make things happen in schools do so "not because of their scientific training and their judicious use of principles of management, but because of their personal and moral presence, their sense of 'what's right,' and their attention to people's needs" (p. 7). Unfortunately, as Dempster et al. found, many principals do value children's well-being above all else, but find those values often inconsistent with the economic rationalism of today's standards-driven schools.

It appears, though, that principals in our study may have been deemed effective largely because they honored their personal moral code. The first standard in the American Association of School Administrators' (2007) code of ethics states, "A school administrator makes the well-being of students the fundamental value of all decision making and actions." A key theme in the data generated by our study is that goals associated with principals' influence strategies truly focus on "what's best for children." It may be that whatever the strategies used, principals' behaviors are ultimately judged against consistency with teachers' values.

Wong (1998) presents a compelling argument that leadership as conceptualized by Burns (1978), Leithwood and Jantzi (2000), Sergiovanni (1992), and others is inherently moral and that moral leadership is no different than the ethical humanism of Confucius. Wong provides a quote attributed to Confucius that could as easily be used to define Leithwood's transformational leaders:

Man of ethical humanity [man of benevolence] must also practice what he has learnt. When he wishes to establish himself, he must at the same time establish others. When he wishes to be prominent, he must also help others to be prominent. [As cited in Chan, 1963, p. 31]

Other parallels between modern Western and early Eastern thinking about education emphasize learning to build character and the belief that everyone is capable of learning. According to Wong (1998), Confucius believed that everyone can succeed through hard work. Not just paying lip service to his "all [children] can learn" belief, Confucius was the first to accept anyone as a pupil, regardless of class. Confucius further believed that the purpose of learning was to bring security and peace to all people. This distinct moral quality of leadership perhaps best describes the leaders our teachers encountered.

THE PERSONALITY OF LEADERS

Effective transformational school leaders are frequently described as optimistic, honest, and considerate. Behaviors such as modeling and visibility convey these values.

Optimism

The positive attitude of principals was noted by several teachers in our study. These principals are perceived as enjoying their jobs and believing in the abilities of their staffs. They also are described as problem solvers who had particularly good relationships with their faculties and students. Teachers reported increases in self-esteem, security, and motivation resulting from principals' optimism. Some indicated that their attitudes also became more positive:

> She has a very positive feeling about our school. She enjoys her job and it is reflected to the rest of the teachers. . . . She faces every day as a new day with new challenges. I try to do the same. I don't mind coming to school this year. When the alarm goes off, I'm "up and at them" this year.

Extra effort was reported by other teachers: "The strategy makes me give 100 percent effort to the school and my class." Another summarized the benefits of a positive approach: "It makes me feel good about what I do."

Martin Seligman (1991), a noted psychologist, is careful to define optimism as the power of nonnegative thinking, not as unjustifiable positivity. The optimist avoids catastrophizing; in times of adversity, consequences are not distorted and are not seen as insurmountable. Thus, the school principal who sees education as being in a state of crisis is neither positive nor negative. The optimist will explain the causes of the crisis in terms that are external, specific, and temporary. The pessimist will explain the crisis as internal ("I should have done more"), pervasive (e.g., "teachers are less competent than they used to be"), and permanent. By monitoring our explanations of the events in our lives, Seligman claims, we can learn to be more optimistic.

Seligman (1991) presents forceful research evidence to suggest that optimists are happier and healthier and live longer than pessimists. More relevant to the present discussion, optimists tend to be liked more and are more successful in their work. Through analysis of campaign speeches, for example, Seligman and his colleagues found that successful United States presidential candidates tend to be more optimistic than their opponents. Our findings confirm that optimism may indeed be a significant factor in leader effectiveness. Seligman, Steen, Park, and Peterson (2005) confirmed through randomized controlled trials that optimism can be learned and sustained. If optimism is a "learnable" behavior, this important leadership characteristic should be part of university coursework for future educational leaders.

Honesty

As used by teachers in our study, honesty refers to the principal's truthfulness, as well as openness and consistency between words and actions. One teacher explained: "There is no phony baloney. . . . She [the principal] will not tell you one thing and do another." Honesty was noted in principals' ability to communicate straightforwardly both positive and negative feedback to teachers. Honest principals confront teachers' weaknesses and acknowledge their strengths. Starratt (2005) identified three virtues of moral leadership: presence, authenticity, and responsibility. It is his third virtue that our teachers described. Starratt says that we are authentic when we are true to ourselves and others. Authenticity is a dialogical relationship which teachers both appreciated and emulated:

Our principal is totally honest in his dealings with the faculty. He is direct with what he feels are our strengths and weaknesses and is always willing to help solve any problem that might arise. . . . [This] keeps me open-minded in my dealings with my students . . . and others on the faculty.

Bryk and Schneider (2002) found that effective transformational principals build "relational trust" in their schools. Nonmanipulation of teachers is viewed as a dimension of social trust that fosters collaboration among our teachers: "I feel that the principal is working with me and I with him, not for him." Teacher satisfaction and effort also are associated with honesty: "You enjoy working for people of this nature, thus you want to improve."

Consideration

Consideration has been recognized as a major dimension of leader behavior in most theories of organizational effectiveness. Alternately termed *people orientation* or *concern for people*, consideration is reported to be related to employee satisfaction by most major leadership theorists (see, e.g., Bass, 1990; Blake & Mouton, 1964; Fiedler, 1967; Hersey & Blanchard, 1977; Stogdill, 1963). In a major study of school effectiveness, Uline, Miller, and Tschannen-Moran (1998) measured two aspects of school effectiveness: instrumental and expressive functions. Expressive functions affect a school's social cohesion and build school culture. Activities associated with trust, teacher and student commitment, and morale are considered expressive activities. These researchers found that both expressive and instrumental activities are significantly correlated with overall school effectiveness and student achievement. Similarly, the Leithwood and Jantzi (2000) factor of "developing people" includes showing intellectual support, giving individualized support, and modeling. Leithwood et al. (1996b) link developing people to school improvement.

Our teachers found that their principals helped them develop by exhibiting a sincere interest in "teachers as human beings." A considerate principal was described as one who "shows a genuine concern for how I am doing . . . [one who] makes a point to say hello." Considerate principals were viewed as nondiscriminating; they showed concern for all teachers. They expressed interest in their teachers' lives during both happy and sad events. One high school teacher gave an example:

> *My principal was very understanding and flexible the times that I had to be absent due to hospitalization of family members. His cooperation and attempts to make my return to school smoother were above and beyond the call of duty. I feel that I've been treated with kindness and respect. I, in turn, tend to have a more compassionate attitude toward my students and their individual situations.*

Effects associated with consideration include enhanced self-esteem ("If he believes in me then I can believe in myself") and improved performance ("I come early and stay late and do maximum work because I know my work is appreciated"). Considerate principals serve as models for teachers. Several teachers reported becoming more considerate and empathic in their dealings with children and fellow teachers. Thus, principals serve as mirrors of appropriate human interaction:

- "Teachers act more as friends, helpers, and resource persons. Students know we care about them and provide encouragement for them to meet their daily challenges."
- "[The principal's consideration] helps to promote warmth in our faculty. We cooperate with each other and express concern for each other."
- "Because our principal shows caring and concern, I feel the need to reciprocate; I want to give him back what he gives us."

PERSONALITY MANIFESTED: MIRRORING THE POSSIBLE

The optimism, honesty, and consideration of effective principals are revealed in their daily interactions with students and teachers. These traits reflect the principals' values. As such, effective teachers also are expected to be optimistic, honest, and considerate. The principals described in our study offer countless opportunities for teachers to acquire similar values by revealing themselves as mirrors to the possible. Effective principals are highly visible and serve as models of appropriate attitudes and behaviors.

Modeling

In earlier chapters, we discuss how effective principals encourage participation by participating as equal members in groups of teachers. As promoters of teacher development, they themselves are avid readers of professional literature, seeking new means of improvement. Expecting teachers to use positive disciplinary approaches with students, they provide examples of such techniques. At times, they also demonstrate teaching techniques. Thus, modeling is used quite effectively to reinforce other strategies of influence.

Modeling as a general influence strategy was recognized by several teachers in the study. Modeling also is a key factor of transformational leadership in numerous studies of principals' effectiveness (Leithwood, Tomlinson, & Genge, 1996a; Leithwood et al., 2004b). Principals enact their expectations for teacher performance through their own behavior. As one teacher explained, "My principal seems to administer by behavior [rather than by] policy. For example, he asks that we dress professionally, monitor the halls between classes, attend extracurricular activities, and contribute to the United Way. He does all of these." Another explained:

> *[My principal] is a very positive person. She conveys her feelings about school and the kids to us without being overbearing or obnoxious. She does not ask us to do anything she has not already done herself or would not do. She does not complain about things that she cannot change. She makes the best of all*

situations. She is a good role model. When I get angry about
something, I think about how she would handle the situation.

Expected behaviors modeled by the principals include appropriate dress, punctuality, effective teaching, positive discipline, praise for students, and extra effort. Without exception, teachers reported that modeling influences them to behave in ways consistent with the principal's implicit expectations. With regard to extra effort, for example, a teacher commented that "many of [the principal's] requests might be viewed as beyond the call of duty, but, because of the principal's modeling, they seem to be part of the job." Another remarked that she tried approaches to student behavior in the hallways that she had seen her principal use effectively. Overall, teachers reported that modeling is a highly effective strategy of influence that leaves them feeling "comfortable," "proud," "aware" (of alternative techniques), and "positive."

Visibility

As a principal's visibility increases, so too do his or her opportunities to model effective behavior. According to our teachers, some principals clearly are more comfortable in hallways and classrooms than in their offices.

Sheppard (1996) synthesizes the research on instructional leadership behaviors, especially those linked to student achievement outcomes. Sheppard confirms a strong positive relationship between leadership behaviors exhibited by principals, such as maintaining high visibility, and teacher commitment, professional involvement, and innovativeness. Similarly, from a study of teachers throughout the United States, Blase and Blase (2004) found that principal visibility led to significant increases in teacher motivation, self-esteem, sense of security, morale, and, to a lesser degree, teacher reflection.

Andrews and Soder (1987) relate gains in mathematics and reading scores of low-achieving students to four instructional leadership roles: instructional resource, resource provider, communicator, and visible presence. In later work, visibility was found to be particularly influential when new programs or techniques are being implemented

(Bamburg & Andrews, 1989). As Kouzes and Posner (1990) observe, "[leaders] demonstrate what is important by how they spend their time, by the priorities on their agenda, by the questions they ask, by the people they see, the places they go, and the behaviors and results that they recognize and reward" (p. 200).

School learning walks have become a popular tool principals use to both show support and monitor progress. Also termed "walk throughs" and "data in a day," learning walks entail short visits to many classrooms (Richardson, 2001). They create a sense of normalcy around observation and open dialog between teachers and administrators.

Our teachers reported that effective principals are visible, both in the hallways and in classrooms. Different goals are attributed to visibility in each setting. Visibility in the hallways is deemed to be an effective manner of communicating support to both teachers and students. Implicit in the principal's presence is an expectation for appropriate student behavior between classes and an offer of assistance to teachers in matters of discipline should they so desire. Visibility in the classroom is associated more typically with expectations for instruction. Expectations for the use of allocated instructional time are implied by the principal's presence, as are expectations regarding implementation of specific instructional strategies. One elementary teacher described her principal's influence through visibility:

> *The principal is extremely involved with all grades and their curricula. She visits the classrooms regularly (two times per week) to make sure that all teachers are on task. She walks around to see if the children are involved and participating in that particular subject. If not, she would place her hands on their shoulders to get their attention and make sure that they are then attentive. This type of discipline is very effective for all children.*

The teachers experienced visibility as positive and nonthreatening. They indicated that visibility in the hallways helps to preempt some discipline problems: "It helps him to see problems before they snowball into serious ones." The principal's presence also affords the opportunity to model optimism: "My principal frequently roams the halls during breaks between classes. He is very friendly and supportive. His positive attitude overflows both to students and to faculty."

Classroom visibility is sporadic for some of the principals and routine for others; some inform teachers of classroom visits, whereas others drop in unannounced. The length of classroom visits also varies widely, as reported in our study, from a few minutes to a whole class period. Some principals walk around the class to "see what the students are busy doing." Others become more fully involved with the class activity: "She visits my class while we are doing laboratory activities . . . participates with the students . . . asks them questions . . . asks me questions. She demonstrates to the students that learning is a lifelong activity."

Teachers indicated that principals usually provide some form of feedback to teachers after visiting their classrooms, also a component of learning walks as described by Richardson (2001). Consistent with the strategy of suggestion discussed in Chapter 7, feedback is presented as advisory. The teachers view visibility as an effective and acceptable strategy because it is accompanied by genuine interest and support. It is not viewed as obtrusive or punitive. Instead, the teachers associate visibility with opportunities for improvement ("You can correct weak points with her help") and increased accountability ("Even though I am a conscientious teacher, I need monitors. Unscheduled pop-in visits are motivational.").

The motivational effect of principals' visibility in the classroom is quite powerful. Numerous examples suggest that although anxiety levels are heightened somewhat by the principal's visit, teachers work harder, are more innovative, and feel better about their own performance as a result:

- "As much as [visits] scare me, I like them because they bring me back to task."
- "Not knowing when I might be visited, I stay on task more often than I might if these visits didn't occur."
- "I try things I previously frowned on—outside labs, field trips."

- "[The principal's visits] caused me to think more about my class and my role as a teacher. I am aware that I am accountable for performance."

MIRRORS SELDOM LIE

We have presented three personality traits—honesty, consideration, and optimism—that appear to be common to effective transformational principals. These traits are evident in principals' frequent interactions with their staffs (i.e., in their visibility) and in the consistency between their expectations and their own actions (i.e., modeling). If modeling and visibility are particularly effective in producing desirable outcomes in teachers for honest, caring, and positive principals, the implications for schools led by manipulative, inconsiderate, and negative principals are terrifying. Principals in the middle—those whose values are less explicit, who are sometimes thoughtful and positive, sometimes distant and gloomy—also emit constant messages to teachers. Teachers learn to be guarded and protective, afraid to trust the unpredictable. The implications for principals are weighty indeed.

Leaders may serve as mirrors to what is possible and what is right for the individuals they serve. But mirrors also can reflect barriers to human potential—lack of trust, feeling, and hope. As all of us who have stopped counting birthdays will attest, mirrors seldom lie. What is reflected to the observer is what the observer has become. If principals are reliable mirrors of what schools will become, we must develop moral leaders. Our data suggest that moral leaders abide by these principles.

1. Do not become so concerned with becoming effective as to ignore the affective.

   Consideration of others—an ethic of caring—is fundamental to moral leadership. Although this aspect of leadership can be improved through careful attention to others, the implications for leader selection should be obvious. Attention to moral fortitude should precede all other qualifications, including demonstrated mastery of certain managerial and instructional skills, in the selection of school leaders.

2. Practice being more optimistic.

According to Seligman (1991), a more positive attitude can be acquired by monitoring our explanations of life's successes and failures. Specifically, we must learn to recognize that adversity is usually temporary, specific, and externally created. Although learning to become more optimistic is a difficult task, its advantages are clearly documented.

3. Be visible, but beware the power of the mirror.

Effective leaders know that their behavior is regarded as the standard of performance. They therefore avail themselves of all opportunities to model the behaviors they expect in others. To become mirrors to what is right and possible, they must ensure that their behavior is above reproach. They must be honest in their interactions with others; the values they convey must be consistent in words and actions as well as over time. As long as principals are in contact with teachers, they are transmitting their values and expectations. The burden of the mirror is that it never stops reflecting.

CHAPTER TEN

Conclusions, Caveats, and Challenges

> *To change our guidance program, the principal involved the faculty in devising a plan. The major input came from the creative and technical talents of the staff. We brainstormed what was wrong with the current situation and described what we wanted. Staff members researched program options and visited schools using the preferred programs . . . . At times in the process I wondered why [the principal] didn't just decide. [Collaborative problem solving] can feel like more work to teachers. But the staff got very excited and very supportive. That was not the case at other schools. By empowering and validating teachers, change occurs, schools become more positive and more effective.*
>
> —An elementary school teacher

In preceding chapters, we describe a number of strategies and related practices that teachers in our study associate with the effectiveness of their principals. We attempted to use the teachers' words as much as possible to portray leader behaviors as teachers themselves view such behaviors. Specific practices reported by teachers are used to elaborate on the use of each strategy. For example, practices associated with the strategy of involvement include an open-door policy, solicitation of suggestions, delegation, and formal team structures. Administrative support ("leading by standing behind") includes providing basic materials, reducing interference of instructional time, paying tuition for professional conferences, and assisting teachers in matters of student discipline.

In all cases, we describe the strategies and tactics that emerged from our data; that is, descriptions of effective principals are accounts of what enhances teaching from the teachers' perspectives. Who better to tell us how to influence teacher performance positively?

Based on teachers' reports, we conclude that principals who are effective:

- Praise teachers' professional accomplishments associated with school goals
- Communicate and model high expectations for student achievement
- Use data to support teacher involvement in *significant* schoolwide decisions
- Grant professional autonomy regarding curriculum and instruction to teachers exhibiting professional readiness
- Support teachers with material resources, protection of instructional time, professional development, and assistance with student discipline and parental concerns
- Encourage individual growth through advice, feedback, and professional development
- Exercise authority as necessary and when justifiable in ethical terms
- Consistently model effective practices congruent with principals' ethical code

Our data indicate that individual principals use most of the strategies we describe and often simultaneously. Further, principals are honest, optimistic, considerate, and highly visible in their schools. They seem to enjoy their work and infect others with a positive outlook.

Teachers reported that these strategies have many positive effects on their thinking, attitudes, and behavior. Most frequently mentioned are enhanced self-esteem and confidence, greater sensitivity to student needs, job satisfaction, commitment and loyalty, flexibility and creativity, extra time and effort, and improved faculty morale.

On the basis of teacher reports, we present suggestions for principals with regard to each successful influence strategy. These are offered only as suggestions and not as prescriptions for effective leader behavior. The reader must cautiously and reflectively consider the applicability of each suggestion in the context of particular school settings. In fact, a small amount of negative data did surface regarding effective principals. In describing strategies used by principals to influence their behavior, a few teachers reported that their effective principals occasionally use coercion or authoritarianism to gain their compliance. It should also be stressed that teachers rated these strategies as very ineffective. When used, they provoked resistance or alienation in teachers.

CONTEXTUAL, REFLECTIVE LEADERSHIP

Our findings are generally consistent with other research on effective principals (e.g., Barth, 1990; Leithwood et al., 2004a, 2004b). Still, there is much debate about what constitutes effective practice in educational administration (Stewart, 2006). For example, principals often find the demands of increased accountability inconsistent with the ideals of restructured and recultured schools.

Some advancements in understanding effective leadership are noteworthy. In 1989, Wimpelberg, Teddlie, and Stringfield (1989) argued that what little we know about effective schools had not been examined through different contextual lenses. Leithwood et al. (2004a, 2004b) later expanded their process of identifying school, classroom, and teacher conditions that interact with leadership practices.

Because problems and contexts are idiosyncratic, it is not possible to tell principals specifically what to do to promote successful teaching. How does the practitioner know when to use particular strategies? Schön (1983, 1991) noted that some professions, particularly in the social sciences, do not conform to preexisting understandings of professional practice. Rules and procedures cannot be specified a priori for all problems of practice. Instead, problems are unique; their resolution must be determined "on the spot." The practitioner must almost simultaneously frame the problem, determine alternative courses of action, choose from among the alternatives, apply and test one solution, and then re-frame and retest based on the results. Schön calls this process "reflection in action."

In organizations as complex and dynamic as schools, events unfold rapidly and new problems continually arise. Problem solving must consist of what Schön (1983) calls a "reflective conversation with the situation" (p. 242), a mental testing of assumptions while activating solutions. In contrast to pure science, no definitive theories or facts capture the reality of schools and allow us to resolve problems easily. Instead, the practitioner must draw on knowledge gained from the theory and research of the profession as well as knowledge acquired through experience. In addition to what they have learned from training and research, principals do have the benefit of experience in specific contexts.

Like Schön, we wish to acknowledge the crucial role that experience and reflection play—indeed must play—in determining how best to lead a school. The reflective practitioner uses both experience and science reflectively in framing and solving unique problems in varying contexts. Of course, many of the behaviors and characteristics that we describe throughout this book would be appropriate to many different situations. One would be hard-pressed to argue that principals should not be honest with teachers or model the behaviors they expect. All strategies require reflection. How often should modeling occur, under what circumstances, and to what degree?

To be applicable in restructured schools, other strategies require more critical reflection. When will praise, for example, be perceived as sincere and motivating, and when will it be perceived as condescending? At least one teacher in our study was angry at her principal's frequent use of praise. She wondered why the principal did not see her as a professional who was motivated by the work itself, with no need for external verbal reinforcement. Each school and each teacher presents a unique context for the person in the formal position of leader. Knowing when a particular set of behaviors is appropriate requires many on-the-spot conversations. No how-to book can alleviate the need for reflection in action—reflection that includes understanding the political, social, and interpersonal dynamics of the situation.

Similarly, no action, once taken, is educative without further reflection on that action and its consequences. Schön (1983) cautions that without both reflection in and on action, professionals resort to routinized performance that is necessarily less effective in new circumstances with new problems of practice. Dewey (1963), too, warns that experience can be "mis-educative" if not followed by deliberate attempts (through reflection) to link the new experience to earlier ones and to other forms of knowledge.

TRANSFORMATIONAL AND MORAL LEADERSHIP

Our research fills a gap in the professional literature on effective principals. Evers and Lakomski (2000) criticized research on transformational leadership as developing factors on the basis of flawed research. They argue that quantitative methods yield time- and place-specific findings that are based on respondents' subjective interpretation of surveys. Quite the contrary, we relied on qualitative methods using grounded theory, as they suggest. Are our findings consistent with the latest quantitative research on transformational leadership? We contend that they are closely matched and that both methods produce more specific leader behaviors that cumulatively paint the picture of the effective principal. To demonstrate, we use the research of Kenneth Leithwood whose surveys resulted in dozens of studies of transformational leadership in numerous settings.

Leithwood and Jantzi (2000) identified three "basics" of successful leadership: setting directions, developing people, and redesigning the organization. They give examples of leadership practices associated with each of the basics. Lending support to their findings and ours is the fact that these practices align quite easily to the leader behaviors we identified through a very different research paradigm.

Consider the table below:

Table 10.1   Effective Leader Behaviors as Transformational

Blase and Kirby Effective Leader Behaviors	Leithwood Transformational Behaviors: Setting Directions	Leithwood Transformational Behaviors: Developing People	Leithwood Transformational Behaviors: Redesigning the Organization
Praise teachers' professional accomplishments congruent with school goals	[Articulate a vision]		[Strengthen culture]
Communicate and model high expectations for student achievement	Create high performance expectations	Provide models of best practices and organizational values	
Use data to support teacher involvement in *significant* schoolwide decisions	Foster acceptance of group goals		Build collaborative processes
Grant professional autonomy regarding curriculum and instruction to teachers exhibiting professional readiness		Provide intellectual stimulation	[Strengthen culture]
Support teachers with material resources, protection of instructional time, professional development, and assistance with student discipline and parental concerns		Provide individualized support	
Encourage individual growth through advice, feedback, and professional development		Provide intellectual stimulation	[Modify structures]
Exercise authority as necessary and when justifiable in ethical terms			[Strengthen culture]
Consistently model effective practices congruent with principals' ethical code	[Articulate a vision]	Provide models of best practices and organizational values	

Other than Leithwood and Jantzi's "strengthen culture" behavior and our "praise" recommendation, the two frameworks are clearly aligned. We would contend that strengthening culture is more of a construct than a behavior which is why it is more difficult to recognize in our data. Nevertheless, all of our recommendations together would transform the culture of a school, as many of our principals noted.

In addition to being "transforming" behaviors, we find that the practices we recommend are embedded in a moral code. Many principals talked about the values held by their leaders. We wondered then how our behaviors aligned with the AASA's (2007) Code of Ethics for Educational Leaders, as well as with the standards and domains of the Interstate School Leaders Licensure Consortium (ISLLC) (Council of Chief State School Officers, 1996) and the National Policy Board for Educational Administration's (NPBEA) Educational Leaders Constituent Council (ELCC, 2002) currently under revision (NPBEA, 2007). The ISLLC standards are national models for state policies regarding certification and licensure. They were adapted or adopted by 41 states by 2005. The ELCC based its standards for university leadership preparation programs on the ISLLC standards. They were adopted for use in the NCATE accreditation process. The Council of Chief State School Officers funded revision of both the ISLLC and ELCC/NCATE standards in 2006.

The AASA Code of Ethics (adopted March 1, 2007) lists twelve behaviors of the ethical school leader. The first three include qualities frequently mentioned by our teachers in describing their effective principals. They are honesty, integrity, holding the well-being of students above all else, and protecting the rights of all individuals. Also seen in our data were behaviors 9 (continuous professional growth) and 12 (service to others above self). The remaining seven behaviors of the AASA Code were less frequently found in our data because they are less likely to be viewed as influencing teachers. These include, for example, adherence to law and policy, advocating for correction of policies deemed inconsistent with educational goals, honoring contracts, and accepting responsibility for actions.

The ISLLC (1996, 2007 draft revision) and ELCC (2002) frameworks include six common standards. ELCC includes Internship as Standard 7 specifically for university preparation programs. The first common standard is developing and sustaining a school vision conducive to professional growth and student learning. This includes creating, implementing, and evaluating plans that promote student success. These behaviors are clearly embedded in Leithwood's "Redesigning the organization" behaviors and in our communicating high expectations for student achievement and using data to support teacher involvement in schoolwide decisions.

The second ISLLC/ELCC standard advocates creating a culture of professional growth and student achievement. Standard 3 deals with management issues, including provision of resources for a safe and effective learning environment. Standard 4 requires collaboration with teachers and the community. Although not evident in our teacher-specific research, Leithwood does address how the effective principal mobilizes community support (Leithwood et al., 2004b).

Standard 5 encompasses the AASA moral code, stating that school leaders should promote student success by acting with integrity, fairness, and in an ethical manner. Like Standard 4, Standard 6 concerns issues not addressed by our research but clear in Leithwood's context factors and AASA's Code. It conveys the need for principal advocacy in political, legal, social, economic, and cultural contexts that affect education.

We compare the ISLLC and ELCC standards to our research findings to demonstrate similarities and differences. Our intent is to present the latest thinking on effective, transformational, ethical principal behavior with the hope that the reader takes away concrete examples of ways to bring about critical school improvement. None of these lists is better or worse, and none are contradictory. Instead, they work together to provide a still incomplete, but increasingly persuasive body of skills, attitudes, and behaviors of exemplary school leaders.

Table 10.2   Effective Leader Behaviors and Leadership Standards

Blase and Kirby Effective Leader Behaviors	ISLLC/ELCC School Leadership Standards
Praise teachers' professional accomplishments congruent with school goals	1. Facilitates development, articulation, implementation, and stewardship of a vision of student success
Communicate and model high expectations for student achievement	2. Advocates for, creates, and sustains a school culture conducive to student learning and staff professional growth
Use data to support teacher involvement in *significant* schoolwide decisions	4. Collaborate with faculty [and community] to promote student success 1. One example under Standard 1 is use of data in support of vision
Grant professional autonomy regarding curriculum and instruction to teachers exhibiting professional readiness	[Tangentially related to developing the instructional capacity of staff, an example of Standard 2]
Support teachers with material resources, protection of instructional time, professional development, and assistance with student discipline and parental concerns	3. Manage organization, operations, and resources for effective learning environment 2. Advocates for, creates, and sustains a school culture conducive to student learning and staff professional growth
Encourage individual growth through advice, feedback, and professional development	2. Advocates for, creates, and sustains a school culture conducive to student learning and staff professional growth
Exercise authority as necessary and when justifiable in ethical terms	5. Acts fairly, ethically, and with integrity
Consistently model effective practices consistent with principals' ethical code	5. Acts fairly, ethically, and with integrity
[Not related directly to teacher behavior; therefore, not addressed in this research]	6. Advocates for students in political, social, economic, legal, and cultural contexts

REFLECTIONS ON THE FUTURE

Leithwood et al. (2004a) conclude that "Leadership is second only to classroom instruction among all school-related factors that contribute to what students learn in school" (p. 5). If teacher behaviors carry primary weight and leaders secondary, then the behaviors of leaders to motivate teachers for school improvement are doubly important. The literature on leadership in restructuring schools offers much hope for a demoralized teaching profession. Although the efforts of school reformers are generally sincere, and the commitment of school practitioners to new processes of governance is authentic, such change in schools presents all concerned parties with a number of profound challenges. What will constitute effective and dynamic leadership in the schools of the future? What kinds of leadership purposes and strategies will help facilitate the transformation from bureaucratic to shared governance structures? If administrators do not support change, or if their actions are even unintentionally inconsistent with the intended goals and processes, such change will likely fail. Can the knowledge gleaned from leader behaviors in the schools studied today assist us in preparing leaders for the schools of tomorrow?

What are some basic assumptions regarding leadership in restructured schools? First, the formal authority of administrators would be diminished. Instead, their role would become increasingly facilitative; they would help provide the basic resources and avenues for teachers to accomplish the goals and objectives that are collectively determined. As such, strategies of influence—such as authority as we discuss it—probably would be less viable.

A second assumption about leadership in restructured schools is that a key role of administrators would become helping teachers to become leaders. Many administrators already use the strategy of involving teachers in decision making. Such involvement may be the first step toward greater teacher leadership. Delegation is one technique for involving teachers; unfortunately, though, many principals delegate to only a handful of teachers. As Roland Barth (1988) notes:

> A powerful relationship exists between learning and leading. . . .
> This is where teacher leadership intersects with professional

development. Teachers who assume responsibility for something they care desperately about—a new pupil-evaluation system, revising the science curriculum, or setting up that computer lab—stand at the gate of profound learning. (1990, ¶ 7)

Thus, it appears that involvement must be accompanied by continuous and meaningful professional development to be successful in achieving the goals of restructured schools—that is, of making teachers into leaders.

Although there are no easy recipes for effective leadership in restructured schools, perhaps we can begin to identify a framework to assist principals in developing a leadership approach that is most appropriate. To begin, administrators have to evaluate both the purposes and the strategies they use in their work with teachers. Do such purposes treat teachers as coleaders, or is there an underlying attempt to control teachers? Do the strategies facilitate teacher growth and professional development in ways that are consistent with teachers' needs and aspirations? In effect, are principals working with teachers to ensure that the ends of education (goals, purposes, etc.) and the means of education emerge from collaborative interaction with teachers?

We believe that two conditions are necessary for the successful restructuring of schools. The first is the kind of transformational leadership that many principals are beginning to learn. According to Burns (1978) and Leithwood et al. (2004b), transformational leaders help develop followers through individualized attention to their professional growth and challenges to the existing order. In schools, this would require viable alternatives to the traditional faculty in-service; individual needs are seldom met through activities designed for all. It would also require that needs and goals be mutually determined. Although some administrators will form committees for strategic planning and staff development, many will do so only in response to the moving pendulum. Their commitment is to improve perceptions, not to develop teachers. Our study suggests that many effective principals are committed to teacher development and collective decision making. The use of strategies such as involvement and support for teachers to attend professional functions indicates a move in the direction of transformational leadership.

The second condition necessary for successful restructuring is teachers' commitment to expanded roles and to increased accountability. Of course, teacher commitment is directly related to leader intent. If the principal and other school and district administrators are perceived as "playing at" restructuring, teachers are unlikely to invest their time and energy in the game. If, however, teachers view the efforts as sincere and accept the challenge to become partners in school leadership, then the likelihood of real transformation improves. Many of the leaders described to us were perceived as honest and sincere in their commitment to school improvement. These personal characteristics that teachers associate with effective principals appear to be necessary qualities of leaders in restructured/ transformed schools.

We believe that administrators have an obligation to provide opportunities for teacher growth, but we also hold teachers accountable for seizing those opportunities. Only by virtue of their expanded commitment and knowledge do teachers earn access to decision-making power. Teachers have traditionally been afforded access to neither decision-making nor individual learning opportunities. Paradoxically, once teachers are able and willing to assume leadership functions in schools, it would be unlikely that they could ever again be disempowered.

At this important juncture in the history of American education, school administrators face enormous challenges. Teacher leadership may be viewed as key to improving the academic and social opportunities for students. Conversely, it might be viewed as a threat to the continuation of the principalship. Whether the school leaders of today view restructuring as a threat to their survival or as a promise for optimizing student growth depends largely on their own values and character. Whether they "play at" restructuring or earnestly attempt transformation will depend on their political orientations and confidence in teachers. Our data suggest that many principals have already accepted the challenge to reform schools. For others who are also sincere in their efforts to improve education for all participants, we offer the strategies of effective transformational principals leading today's schools—those pioneers who must balance simultaneous and conflicting external pressures both to control and to empower—as backdrops for reflective practice.

Resource

Research Methods
and Procedures

The purpose of this book has been to focus on issues of practice. Some readers may be interested in a detailed account of how the data on which the book is based were collected and analyzed, however. A brief description is provided herewith.

Procedures for data collection and analysis were based in symbolic interaction theory. This methodological perspective emphasizes the interpretations and meanings that people construct in their particular social settings. The individual is viewed as a social product who is influenced by external factors (e.g., policies, superordinate leadership) but who also is capable of maintaining distance and is able to initiate individual action (Blumer, 1969; Mead, 1934). In contrast to some qualitative research perspectives, symbolic interactionism focuses on the structure of individual consciousness and perceptions (Blumer, 1969; Tesch, 1988).

Using this method, the study reported in this book employed open-ended questions and focused on the broad question, "What are teachers' definitions of the strategies school principals use to influence them?" Descriptive data relevant to understanding teachers' perspectives were collected.

The importance of perceptions to the topics identified previously is well established in the leadership, micropolitics, and organizational power literature (Bacharach & Lawler, 1980; Ball, 1987; Burns, 1978; Hamilton & Biggart, 1985; Mangham, 1979; Pfeffer, 1981). The data were analyzed to generate categories, themes, conceptual understandings, and theoretical ideas.

Allport (1942) suggests that an open-ended questionnaire is a useful personal document for qualitative research that focuses on the subjective perceptions of people. Such an instrument is defined as "any self-revealing document that intentionally or unintentionally yields information regarding the structure, dynamics, and functioning of the author's life" (p. xii). A *questionnaire* is defined as a personal document when the research participants exercise substantial control over the content of their responses. Questionnaires of this type have been employed successfully in other research (Blase, 1986, 1988; Blase & Pajak, 1986; Pajak & Blase, 1989).

An open-ended questionnaire, the Inventory of Strategies Used by Principals to Influence Teachers (ISUPIT), was designed to elicit free expression of personal meanings regarding the research topic. To develop the first version of the ISUPIT, the researcher consulted with a committee of three professors and five teachers. This instrument was piloted with 39 graduate students enrolled in education courses at a major state university. Suggestions made by the committee and students were considered in the construction of the final form of the instrument.

The ISUPIT consisted of three legal-size pages. On the first page, teachers provided general background information. They also rated their principals in terms of openness and effectiveness (on seven-point scales). On two additional pages, teachers were asked to provide detailed descriptions of two influence strategies used by their school principals. The specific questions were:

1. Describe and give a detailed example of a strategy or tactic (overt or covert; formal or informal; positive or negative) that your principal uses frequently to influence what you *do* or *think* in the school or in the classroom.

2. Describe and give an example of the *effects* (impact) that the strategy has on your *thinking* and *behavior* (if any).

3. Describe and illustrate what you believe to be your principal's *goals/purposes* in using the strategy identified above.

4. How *effective* is the strategy in getting you to think and do what the principal intended? (seven-point scale) Please explain why.

5. What *feelings* (if any) do you have about your principal's use
of this strategy?

Exploratory research of this nature is designed to produce data-based categories and conceptual understandings by increasing the variation among the research participants (Bogdan & Taylor, 1975; Glaser, 1978; Glaser & Strauss, 1967). Because of the open-ended design of the ISUPIT, the substantial time required for completion (about 40 minutes), and the sensitivity of the research topic to practitioners, a mailout survey was ruled out. Rather, 14 professors of education administered the ISUPIT between 1989 and 1990 to full-time public school teachers taking courses in five on- and off-campus centers of universities located in one southeastern, one northeastern, and one northwestern state. Involvement in this study was voluntary; teachers were not instructed to write their names on the research instrument.

Of the more than 1,200 respondents who completed the ISUPIT, 836 identified their principals as open, effective, and participatory on the seven-point scales provided (means were 5.7, 5.9, and 5.2, respectively). The remaining teachers described influence strategies used by principals who were perceived as relatively closed and ineffective. *This book presents only the open-effective portion of the data* ($n = 836$). The decision to discuss this portion of the database was founded on its theoretical, research, and practical significance.

The primary sample consisted of male ($n = 172$) and female ($n = 664$) teachers from rural ($n = 292$), suburban ($n = 443$), and urban ($n = 101$) school locations. Elementary ($n = 335$), junior/ middle ($n = 284$), and high school teachers ($n = 217$) participated. The average age of teachers was 37; the average years in teaching was 12. The sample included tenured ($n = 714$) and nontenured ($n = 122$) teachers. Married ($n = 669$), single ($n = 130$), and divorced teachers ($n = 37$) participated. Degrees earned were BA /BS ($n = 299$), MEd/MA/MS/EdS ($n = 523$), and EdD/PhD ($n = 14$). The teachers described male ($n = 497$) and female principals ($n = 339$). The mean number of years with the current principal at the time of this study was four.

The study sample is roughly consistent with the national distribution of teachers in terms of gender, age, degrees earned, and marital status. A slightly lower percentage of average years of experience, a lower percentage from urban locations and higher percentage from suburban locations, a lower percentage from elementary schools and higher percentage from junior/middle and high schools were represented in the sample, compared with the national distribution (National Education Association, 1983, 1990).

Data from the subsample of 836 teachers were coded according to principles for comparative analysis (Glaser, 1978; Glaser & Strauss, 1967). This procedure consisted of a comparison of each element coded previously in terms of emergent categories and subcategories. Line-by-line analysis of each questionnaire page (which included descriptions) produced 1,323 major strategies and a host of tactics (i.e., specific practices) related to each strategy. Subsequently, each strategy was analyzed within the context of the questionnaire items on the ISUPIT. That is, data related to effects on teacher thinking/behavior, principals' goals, effectiveness of strategies, and feelings were coded for categories and subcategories. Display matrices synthesizing each aspect of each strategy then were constructed (Miles & Huberman, 1984). These charts facilitated numerical analyses of strategies as well as further substantive analyses (e.g., effects on teachers). Comparisons across strategies were used to construct data-based conceptual and theoretical statements.

Each of the two questionnaire pages available to respondents was analyzed for only one strategy. In essence, the number of strategies coded is equal to the number of pages completed. In all, 836 teachers described 1,323 strategies used by principals with whom they worked and who they believed were open and effective.

The database was also inspected to determine if the use of certain influence strategies was linked to such characteristics as gender of the principals or teachers. Although discernible patterns were generated from this analysis, no conclusions were drawn.

One researcher analyzed the questionnaire data. This required approximately 800 hours. In addition, three professors and two doctoral students were consulted when questions arose. The doctoral students also inspected the descriptive matrices developed by the researcher. As noted, each matrix was designed to display different segments of raw data, thematic data, and data related to theoretical codes.

Consistent with the principles for inductive analysis, all the descriptive categories, themes, and conceptual ideas presented in this book were derived from data appearing on the ISUPIT.

References

Ackerman, R. H., Donaldson, G. A., & van der Bogert, R. (1996). *Making sense as a school leader: Persisting questions, creative opportunities.* San Francisco: Jossey-Bass.

Allen, L., Glickman, C., & Hensley, F. (1998, April). *A search for accountability: The League of Professional Schools.* Paper presented at the annual meeting of the American Educational Research Association, San Diego.

Allport, G. (1942). *The use of personal documents in psychological science.* New York: Social Science Research Council.

American Association of School Administrators. (2007). *AASA's statement of ethics for school leaders.* Arlington, VA: Author.

Andrews, R. L., & Soder, R. (1987). Principal instructional leadership and school achievement. *Instructional Leadership, 44,* 9–11.

Argyris, C. (1957). *Personality and organization.* New York: Harper & Row.

Armor, D., Congry-Oseguera, P., Cox, M., King, N., McDonnell, L., Pascal, A., Pauly, E., & Zellman, G. (1976). *Analysis of the school-preferred reading program in selected Los Angeles minority schools.* Santa Monica, CA: RAND.

Aryee, S., & Stone, R. J. (1996). Work experiences, work adjustments, and psychological well-being of expatriate employees in Hong Kong. *The International Journal of Human Resource Management, 7,* 150–164.

Bacharach, S. B., & Lawler, E. J. (1980). *Power and politics in organizations: The social psychology of conflict, coalitions, and bargaining.* San Francisco: Jossey-Bass.

Bacharach, S. B., Bamberger, P., Conley, S. C., & Bauer, S. (1990). The dimensionality of decision participation in educational organizations. *Educational Administration Quarterly, 26,* 126–167.

Ball, S. J. (1987). *The micro-politics of the school: Towards a theory of school organization.* London: Methuen.

Bamburg, J., & Andrews, R. (1989). School goals, principals, and achievement. *School Effectiveness and School Improvement, 2*(3), 175–191.

Bandura, A. (1986). *Social foundations of thought and action.* Englewood Cliffs, NJ: Prentice-Hall.

Barth, R. S. (1990). *The teacher leader.* Retrieved June 20, 2008 from http://www.edutopia.org/teacher-leader

Bass, B. M. (1985). *Leadership and performance beyond expectations.* New York: Free Press.

Bass, B. M. (1988). Evolving perspectives on charismatic leadership. In J. A. Conger & R. N. Kanungo (Eds.), *Charismatic leadership: Behind the mystique of exceptional leadership* (pp. 40–77). San Francisco: Jossey-Bass.

Bass, B. M. (1990). *Bass and Stogdill's handbook of leadership: Theory, research, and managerial applications* (2nd ed.). New York: Free Press.

Beatty, B. R. (2000). The emotions of educational leadership: Breaking the silence. *Instructional Journal of Leadership in Education*, *3*(4), 331–357.

Beck, L. G. (1994). *Reclaiming educational administration as a caring profession.* New York: Teachers College Press.

Beck, L. G., & Murphy, J. (1994). *Ethics in educational leadership programs: An expanding role.* Thousand Oaks, CA: Corwin Press.

Bhuian, S. N., Al-Shammari, E. S., & Jefri, O. A. (1996). Occupational commitment, job satisfaction, and job characteristics: An empirical study of expatriates in Saudi Arabia. *International Journal of Commerce and Management*, *6*, 57–80.

Blake, R., & Mouton, J. (1964). *The managerial grid.* Houston, TX: Gulf.

Blase, J. (1986). A qualitative analysis of sources of teacher stress: Consequences for performance. *American Educational Research Journal*, *23*(1), 13–40.

Blase, J. (1987). Dimensions of effective school leadership: The teachers' perspective. *American Educational Research Journal, 24*(4), 598–610.

Blase, J. (1988). The politics of favoritism: A qualitative analysis of the teachers' perspective. *Educational Administrative Quarterly*, *24*(2), 152–177.

Blase, J., & Anderson, G. (1995). *The micropolitics of educational leadership: From control to empowerment.* London: Caswell.

Blase, J., & Blase, J. (1996). *The fire is back: Principals sharing school governance.* Thousand Oaks, CA: Corwin Press.

Blase, J., & Blase, J. (1998). *Handbook of instructional leadership.* Thousand Oaks, CA: Corwin Press.

Blase, J., & Blase, J. (2001). *Empowering teachers: What successful principals do* (2nd ed.). Thousand Oaks, CA: Corwin Press.

Blase, J., & Blase, J. (2003). *Breaking the silence: Overcoming the problem of principal mistreatment of teachers.* Thousand Oaks, CA: Corwin Press.

Blase, J., & Blase, J. (2004). *Handbook of instructional leadership: How successful principals promote teaching and learning* (2nd ed.). Thousand Oaks, CA: Corwin Press.

Blase, J., & Blase, J. (2006). *Teachers bringing out the best in teachers: A guide to peer consultation for administrators and teachers.* Thousand Oaks, CA: Corwin Press.

Blase, J., & Pajak, E. (1986). The impact of teachers' worklife on personal life: A qualitative analysis. *Alberta Journal of Educational Research*, *32*(4), 307–322.

Blase, J., & Phillips, D. (2008). *Doing what matters: How exemplary principals overcome managerial responsibilities and focus on school improvement.* Athens, GA: The University of Georgia.

Blase, J., & Roberts, J. (1994). The micropolitics of teacher work involvement: Effective principals' impacts on teachers. *Alberta Journal of Educational Research*, *40*(1), 67–94.

Blase, J., Blase, J., Anderson, G., & Dungan, S. (1997). *Democratic principals in action: Eight pioneers.* Thousand Oaks, CA: Corwin Press.

Blumberg, A. (1989). *School administration as a craft: Foundations of practice.* Boston: Allyn & Bacon.

Blumberg, A., & Greenfield, W. (1986). *The effective principal: Perspectives on school leadership* (2nd ed.). Boston: Allyn & Bacon.

Blumer, H. (1969). *Symbolic interactionism: Perspective and method*. Englewood Cliffs, NJ: Prentice Hall.

Bogdan, R., & Taylor, S. (1975). *Introduction to qualitative research methods: A phenomenological approach to the social sciences*. New York: John Wiley.

Bolman, L. G., & Deal, T. E. (1995). *Leading with soul*. San Francisco: Jossey-Bass.

Boris-Schater, S., & Langer, S. (2006). *Balanced leadership: How effective principals manage their work*. New York: Teachers College Press.

Bossert, S., Dwyer, D., Rowan, B., & Lee, G. (1982). The instructional management role of the principal. *Educational Administration Quarterly, 18*(3), 34–64.

Brady, L. (1985). The supportiveness of the principal in school-based curriculum development. *Journal of Curriculum Studies, 17*(1), 95–97.

Bredeson, P. V. (1986, April). *Principally speaking: An analysis of the interpersonal communications of school principals*. Paper presented at the annual meeting of the American Educational Research Association, San Francisco.

Bredeson, P. V. (1995, April). *From gazing out of the ivory towers to heavy lifting in the field: Empowerment through collaborative active research*. Paper presented at the annual meeting of the Philosophy of Education Society, Arlington, VA.

Brookover, W. B., Beady, C., Flood, P., Schweitzer, J., & Wisenbaker, J. (1979). *School social systems and student achievement: Schools can make a difference*. New York: Praeger.

Brookover, W. B., & Lezotte, L. (1977). *Schools can make a difference*. East Lansing: Michigan State University, College of Urban Development.

Bryk, A. S., & Schneider, B. (2002). *Trust in schools: A core resource for improvement*. New York, NY: Russell Sage Foundation.

Burns, J. M. (1978). *Leadership*. New York: Harper & Row.

Capper, C. A., Frattura, E., & Keyes, M. W. (2000). *Meeting the needs of students of all abilities*. Thousand Oaks, CA: Corwin Press.

Cawelti, G. (Ed.). (2004). *Handbook of research on improving student achievement*. Arlington, VA: Educational Research Service.

Chan, W. T. (1963). *A source book in Chinese philosophy*. Princeton NJ: Princeton University Press.

Cibulka, J. G. (2001). The changing role of interest groups in education: Nationalization and the new politics of education productivity. *Educational Policy, 15*(1), 12–40.

Clift, R., Johnson, M., Holland, P., & Veal, M. L. (1992). Developing the potential for collaborative school leadership. *American Educational Research Journal, 29*(4), 877–908.

Colvin, G. (2007). *7 Steps for developing a proactive schoolwide discipline plan: A guide for principals and leaderships teams*. Thousand Oaks, CA: Corwin Press.

Conger, C. L., & Kanungo, R. N. (1998). *Charismatic leadership in organizations*. Thousand Oaks, CA: Sage.

Conger, J. A., & Kanungo, R. N. (1994). Charismatic leadership in organizations: Perceived behavioural attributes and their measurement. *Journal of Organizational Behaviour, 15*, 439–452.

Conley, S., & Bacharach, S. B. (1990, March). From school-site management to participatory school-site management. *Phi Delta Kappan, 71*(7), 539–544.

Council of Chief State School Officers. (1996). *Interstate School Leaders' Licensure Consortium Standards for School Leaders*. Washington, DC: Author.

Crow, G. M., Matthews, L. J., & McCleary, L. E. (1996). *Leadership: A relevant and realistic role for principals*. Princeton, NJ: Eye on Education.

Deal, T. (1987). Effective school principals: Counselors, engineers, pawn brokers, poets . . . or instructional leaders? In W. Greenfield (Ed.), *Instructional leadership: Concepts, issues, and controversies* (pp. 230–245). Boston: Allyn & Bacon.

Deal, T., & Peterson, K. (1990). *The principal's role in shaping school culture*. Washington, DC: Department of Education.

Dembo, M. H., & Gibson, S. (1985). Teachers' sense of efficacy: An important factor in school improvement. *Elementary School Journal, 86*(2), 173–184.

Dempster, N., Freakley, M., & Parry, L. (2001). The ethical climate of public schooling under new public management. *International Journal of Leadership In Education, 4*(1), 1–12.

Donaldson, G. A., Jr. (1990, April). *Principals in transition: Dilemmas in moving from manager to instructional leader*. Paper presented at the annual meeting of the American Educational Research Association, Boston, MA.

Drake, T. L., & Roe, W. H. (2003). *The principalship*. Upper Saddle River, NJ: Merrill/Prentice Hall.

Drucker, P. F., & Senge, P. M. (2001). *Leading in a time of change: What will it take to lead tomorrow?* New York, NY: The Peter F. Drucker Foundation for Nonprofit Management.

Dunlap, D. M., & Schmuck, P. A. (1995). *Women leading in education*. Albany: State University of New York Press.

Edmonds, R. (1979). Effective schools for the urban poor. *Educational Leadership, 37*(1), 15–24.

Edmonds, R. R. (1982). Programs of school improvement: An overview. *Educational Leadership, 40*(3), 4–11.

Elmore, R. (2004). *School reform from the inside out*. Cambridge: Harvard Education Press.

Epstein, J. (2001). *School, family, and community partnerships: Preparing educators and improving schools*. Boulder, CO: Westview Press.

Evers, C. W. (1992). Ethics and ethical leadership: A pragmatic and holistic approach. In P. A. Duignan & R. J. S. MacPherson (Eds.), *Educative Leadership* (pp. 21–43). London: Falmer Press.

Evers, C. W., & Lakomski, G. (1993). Cognition, values, and organizational structure: Hodgkinson in perspective. *Journal of Educational Administration and Foundations, 8*(1), 45–57.

Evers, C. W., & Lakomski, G. (2000). *Doing educational administration: A theory of administrative practice*. NY: Pergamon.

Fiedler, F. (1967). *A theory of leadership effectiveness*. New York: McGraw-Hill.

Firestone, W. A., & Wilson, B. L. (1985). Using bureaucratic and cultural linkages to improve instruction: The principal's contribution. *Educational Administration Quarterly, 21*(2), 7–30.

Foster, C. (2001, Sept/Oct). Why teach? *Stanford Alumni Magazine*. Stanford, CA: Stanford Alumni Association. Retrieved October 1, 2007, from: http://www.stanfordalumni.org/news/magazine/2001/sepoct/features/whyteach.html

Foster, W. (1991, April). *Moral theory, transformation, and leadership in school settings*. Paper presented at the annual meeting of the American Educational Research Association, Chicago, IL.

French, J., & Raven, B. H. (1959). The bases of social power. In D. Cartwright (Ed.), *Studies of social power* (pp. 150–167). Ann Arbor, MI: Institute for Social Research.

French, J. R. P., & Raven, B. H. (1968). Bases of social power. In D. Cartwright & A. Zander (Eds.), *Group dynamics: Research and theory* (pp. 259–270). New York: Harper & Row.

Fullan, M. F. (2005). *Leadership and sustainability: System thinkers in action.* Thousand Oaks, CA: Corwin Press.

Glaser, B. (1978). *Theoretical sensitivity: Advances in the methodology of grounded theory.* Mill Valley, CA: Sociology Press.

Glaser, B. G., & Strauss, A. L. (1967). *The discovery of grounded theory: Strategies for qualitative research.* Chicago: Aldine.

Glenn, B., & McLean, T. (1981). *What works: An examination of effective schools for poor black children.* Cambridge, MA: Center for Law and Education. (ERIC Document Reproduction Service No. ED 216 060)

Glickman, C. D. (1990). Pushing school reform to a new edge: The seven ironies of school empowerment. *Phi Delta Kappan, 72*(1), 68–75.

Glickman, C. D. (1993). *Renewing America's schools: A guide for school-based action.* San Francisco: Jossey-Bass.

Glickman, C. D. (1998). *Education and democracy: The promise of American schools.* San Francisco: Jossey-Bass.

Glickman, C. D., Gordon, S. P., & Ross-Gordon, J. M. (2004). *Supervision and instructional leadership: A developmental approach* (5th ed.). Boston: Allyn & Bacon.

Goldman, P., Dunlap, D., & Conley, D. T. (1991, April). *Administrative facilitation and site-based school reform projects.* Paper presented at the annual meeting of the American Educational Research Association, Chicago, IL.

Goleman, D., Boyatzis, R., & McKee, A. (2002). *Primal leadership: Realizing the power of emotional intelligence.* Boston: Harvard Business School Press.

Graseck, P. (2005). Where's the ministry in education: Attending to the souls of our schools. *Phi Delta Kappan, 86*(5), 373–378.

Greenfield, W. (1987). Moral imagination and interpersonal competence: Antecedents to instructional leadership. In W. Greenfield (Ed.), *Instructional leadership: Concepts, issues, and controversies* (pp. 56–73). Boston: Allyn & Bacon.

Gregory, G. H., & Chapman, C. (2005). *Differentiating instructional strategies: One size doesn't fit all.* Thousand Oaks, CA: Corwin Press.

Gurr, D., Drysdale, L., & Mulford, B. (2006). Models of successful principal leadership. *School Leadership and Management, 26*(4), 371–395.

Hallinger, P. (1989). Developing instructional leadership teams in high schools. In B. Creemers, T. Peters, & D. Reynolds (Eds.), *School efffectiveness and school improvement* (pp. 319–330). Amsterdam: Swets & Zeitlinger.

Hallinger, P., & Heck, R. H. (1996a). Reassessing the principal's role in school effectiveness: A review of empirical research, 1980–1995. *Educational Administration Quarterly, 32*(1), 5–44.

Hallinger, P., & Heck, R. H. (1996b). The principal's role in school effectiveness: An assessment of methodological progress, 1980–1995. In K. Leithwood, J. Chapman, D. Corson, P. Hallinger, & A. Hart (Eds.), *International handbook of educational leadership and administration* (pp. 723–783). Dordrecht, The Netherlands: Kluwer.

Hallinger, P., & Heck, R. (1999). Next generation methods for the study of leadership and school improvement. In J. Murphy & K.S. Louis (Eds.), *Handbook of research on educational administration* (2nd ed., pp. 141–162). San Francisco: Jossey-Bass.

Hallinger, P., & Murphy, J. (1987). Instructional leadership in the school context. In W. Greenfield (Ed.), *Instructional leadership: Concepts, issues, and controversies*. Boston: Allyn & Bacon.

Hallinger, P., & Richardson, D. (1988). Models of shared leadership: Evolving structures and relationships. *Urban Review, 20*(4), 229–245.

Hamilton, G. G., & Biggart, N. W. (1985). Why people obey: Theoretical observations on power and obedience in complex organizations. *Sociological Perspectives, 28*(1), 3–28.

Hannaway, L., & Stevens, K. (1985, April). *The indirect instructional leadership role of a principal*. Paper presented at the annual meeting of the American Educational Research Association, Chicago.

Hanson, M. (1976). Beyond the bureaucratic model: A study of power and autonomy in educational decision making. *Interchange, 7*(1), 27–38.

Harvey, J. B. (1988). The Abilene paradox: The management of agreement. In *The Abilene paradox and other meditations on management* (pp. 13–36). San Diego, CA: University Associates.

Hawley, W. D. (1988). Missing pieces of the educational reform agenda: Or, why the first and second waves may have missed the boat. *Educational Administration Quarterly, 24*, 416–437.

Heck, R. H., Larsen, T. J., & Marcoulides, G. A. (1990). Instructional leadership and school achievement: Validation of a causal model. *Educational Administration Quarterly, 26*(2), 94–125.

Heck, R. H., & Marcoulides, G. A. (1993). Principal leadership behaviors and school achievement. *NASSP Bulletin, 77*(553), 20–28.

Heifetz, R. A. (1998). *Leadership without any answer*. Cambridge, MA: Belknap Press of Harvard University Press.

Henderson, A., & Mapp, K. (2002). *A new wave of evidence: The impact of school, family and community connections on student achievement*. Austin, TX: Southwest Education Development Laboratory.

Hersey, P., & Blanchard, K. (1977). *Management of organizational behavior*. Englewood Cliffs, NJ: Prentice-Hall.

Hersey, P., Blanchard, K., & Johnson, D. (1996). *Management of organizational behavior*. Upper Saddle River, NJ: Prentice-Hall.

Hersey, P., Blanchard, K., & Natemeyer, W. E. (1976). Situational leadership, perception, and the impact of power. *Group and Organization Studies, 4*, 418–428.

High, R., & Achilles, C. M. (1986). An analysis of influence-gaining behaviors of principals in schools of varying levels of instructional effectiveness. *Educational Administration Quarterly, 22*(1), 111–119.

Hipp, K. A., & Bredeson, P. V. (1995). Exploring connections between teacher efficacy and principals' leadership behavior. *Journal of School Leadership, 5*(2), 136–150.

Hodgkinson, C. (1991). *Educational leadership: The moral art*. Albany: State University of New York

Hord, S. M. (1988). The principal as teacher educator. *Journal of Teacher Education, 39*(3), 8–12.

Hord, S. M. (1997). *Professional learning communities: Communities of continuous inquiry and improvement.* Austin, TX: Southwest Educational Development Laboratory.

Hoy, W. K., & Brown, B. L. (1988). Leadership behavior of principals and the zone of acceptance of elementary teachers. *Journal of Educational Administration, 26*(1), 22–38.

Hoy, W. K., & Miskel, C. G. (2005). *Educational administration: Theory, research, and practice* (7th ed.). Boston: McGraw-Hill.

Hoy, W. K., & Sweetland, S. R. (2001). Designing better schools: The meaning and nature of enabling school structure. *Educational Administration Quarterly, 37,* 296–321.

Hoy, W. K., & Woolfolk, A. E. (1993). Teachers' sense of efficacy and the organizational health of schools. *Elementary School Journal, 93,* 356–372.

Isherwood, G. B. (1973). The principal and his authority: An empirical study. *High School Journal, 56*(6), 291–303.

Janis, I. L. (1985). Sources of error in strategic decision making. In J. M. Pennings (Ed.), *Organizational strategy and change* (pp. 157–197). San Francisco: Jossey Bass.

Johnson, N. A. (1984). *The role of the Australian school principal in staff development.* Unpublished master's thesis, University of New England, Armidale, New South Wales.

Johnson, S. M. (2006). *The workplace matters: Teacher quality, retention, and effectiveness.* Working paper. Atlanta: National Education Association Research Department.

Johnston, G. S., & Venable, B. P. (1986). A study of teacher loyalty to the principal: Rule administration and hierarchical influence of the principal. *Educational Administration Quarterly, 22*(4), 4–27.

Joyce, B., & Showers, B. (1995). *Student achievement through staff development: Fundamentals of school renewal* (2nd ed.). White Plains, NY: Longman.

Joyce, B., Weil, M., & Calhoun, E. (2000). *Models of teaching* (6th ed.). Needham Heights, MA: Allyn & Bacon.

Kirby, P. C. (1992). Shared decision making: Moving from concerns about restrooms to concerns about classrooms. *Journal of School Leadership, 2,* 330–344.

Kirby, P. C., Stringfield, S., Teddlie, C., & Wimpelberg, R. (1992). School effects on teacher socialization. *International Journal of School Effectiveness and Improvement, 4,* 187–203.

Knuth, R. K. (2006). The Monday memo. *Principal Leadership, 7*(3), 32–36.

Kouzes, J. M., & Posner, B. Z. (1990). *The leadership challenge: How to get extraordinary things done in organizations.* San Francisco: Jossey-Bass.

Lasserre, C. (1989). *Relationships between selected school context variables and teacher self-efficacy and self-confidence.* Doctoral dissertation, University of New Orleans.

Lawler, E. E., III. (1984). Leadership in participative organizations. In J. G. Hunt, D. Hosking, C. A. Schreisheim, & R. Stewart (Eds.), *Leaders and managers: International perspectives on managerial behavior and leadership.* Elmsford, NY: Pergamon.

Lee, V., Dedick, R., & Smith, J. (1991). The effect of the social organization of schools on teachers' efficacy and satisfaction. *Sociology of Education, 64,* 190–208.

Leithwood, K. (1994). Leadership for school restructuring. *Educational Administration Quarterly, 30*(4), 498–518.

Leithwood, K. (1996). School restructuring, transformational leadership, and the amelioration of teacher burnout. *Anxiety, Stress, & Coping, 9,* 199–215.

Leithwood, K., Begley, P., & Cousins, B. (1990). The nature, causes, and consequences of principals' practices: An agenda for future research. *Journal of Educational Administration, 28*(4), 5–31.

Leithwood, K., Chapman, J., Corson, D., Hallinger, P., & Hart, A. (Eds.). (1996b). *International handbook of educational leadership and administration.* Dordrecht, Netherlands: Kluwer Academic Publishers.

Leithwood, K., & Jantzi, D. (1990, April). *Transformational leadership. How principals can help reform school cultures.* Paper presented at the annual meeting of the American Educational Research Association, Boston, MA.

Leithwood, K., & Jantzi, D. (2000). Principal and teacher leadership effects: A replication. *School Leadership and Management, 20,* 415–434.

Leithwood, K., Jantzi, D., Earl, L., Watson, N., Levin, B., & Fullan, M. (2004a). Strategic leadership for large-scale reform: The case of England's national literacy and numeracy strategy. *Journal of School Management and Leadership, 24*(1), 57–79.

Leithwood, K., Louis, K., Anderson, S. & Wahlstrom, K. (2004b). *How leadership influences student learning.* Minneapolis: Center for Applied Research and Educational Improvement and Toronto: Ontario Institute for Studies in Education at the University of Toronto.

Leithwood, K., Tomlinson, & Genge, M. (1996a). Transformational school leadership. In K. Leithwood, J. Chapman, D. Corson, P. Hallinger, & A. Hart (Eds.), *International handbook of educational leadership and administration* (pp. 785–840). Dordrecht, The Netherlands: Kluwer.

Lieberman, A., & Miller, L. (1984). *Teachers, their world and their work: Implications for school improvement.* Alexandria, VA: Association for Supervision and Curriculum Development.

Lipham, J. (1981). *Effective principal, effective school.* Reston, VA: American Association of School Principals.

Lortie, D. C. (1975). *Schoolteacher: A sociological study.* Chicago: University of Chicago Press.

Maeroff, G. (1993). Team building for school reform. *The School Administrator, 50*(3), 44–47.

Maeroff, G. I. (1988). Blueprint for empowering teachers. *Phi Delta Kappan, 69*(7), 473–477.

Mangham, I. (1979). *The politics of organizational change.* Westport, CT: Greenwood.

Marks, H. M. & Louis, K. S. (1999). Teacher empowerment and the capacity for organizational learning. *Educational Administration Quarterly, 35*(5), 707–750.

Marks, H. M. & Nance, J. P. (2007). Contexts of accountability under system reform: Implications for principal influence on instruction and supervision. *Educational Administration Quarterly, 43*(1), 3–37.

Marshall, C., Patterson, J. A., Rogers, D. L., & Steele, J. R. (1996). Caring as career: An alternative perspective for educational administration. *Educational Administration Quarterly, 32*(2), 271–294.

Marzano, R. J. (1998). *A theory-based meta-analysis of research on instruction.* Aurora, CO: Mid-Continent Research for Education and Learning.

Marzano, R. J. (2000). *A new era of school reform: Going where the research takes us.* Aurora, CO: Mid-Continent Research for Education and Learning.

Marzano, R. J., Gaddy, B. B., & Dean, C. (2000). *What works in classroom instruction.* Aurora, CO: Mid-Continent Research for Education and Learning.

Marzano, R. J., Pickering, D. J., & Pollock, J. E. (2001). *Classroom instruction that works: Research-based strategies for increasing student achievement.* Alexandria, VA: Association for Supervision and Curriculum Development.

Marzano, R. J., Waters, T., & McNulty, B. A. (2005). *School leadership that works: From research to results.* Alexandria, VA: Association for Supervision and Curriculum Development.

Maslow, A. (1970). *Motivation and personality* (2nd ed.). New York: Harper & Row.

McGregor, D. (1960). *The human side of enterprise.* New York: McGraw-Hill.

Mead, G. H. (1934). *Mind, self and society.* Chicago: University of Chicago Press.

Meyer, J. W., & Rowan, B. (1977). Institutionalized organizations: Formal structure as myth and ceremony. *American Journal of Sociology, 83*, 440–463.

Miles, M. B., & Huberman, A. M. (1984). *Qualitative data analysis: A sourcebook of new methods.* Beverly Hills, CA: Sage.

Murphy, J. (2006). A new view of leadership. *Journal of Staff Development, 27*(3), 51–52, 64.

Murphy, J. & Datnow, A. (2003). *Leadership lessons from comprehensive school reform.* Thousand Oaks, CA: Corwin Press.

Murphy, J., & Louis, K. S. (1994). *Reshaping the principalship: Insights from transformational reform efforts.* Thousand Oaks, CA: Corwin Press.

Muth, R. (1973). *Teacher perceptions of power, conflict, and consensus. Administrator's notebook.* Chicago: Midwest Administration Center.

National Association of Elementary School Principals. (2001). *Leading learning communities: Standards for what principals should know and be able to do.* Alexandria, VA: Author.

National Education Association. (1983). *The national teacher opinion poll* [Research memo]. Washington, DC: Author.

National Education Association. (1990). *Estimates of school statistics.* West Haven, CT: Author.

National Policy Board for Educational Administration (NPBEA). (2002). *Standards for Advanced Programs in Educational Leadership.* Retrieved October 20, 2007 from: http://www.npbea.org/ELCC/ELCCStandards%20_5-02.pdf

National Policy Board for Educational Administration (NPBEA) Standards Revision Steering Committee. (2007). *Draft of revised ISLLC Standards.* Retrieved October 20, 2007, from: http://www.principals.org/s_nassp/sec_inside.asp?CID=1298&DID=56055

Nero, A. B. (1985). *Intrinsic and extrinsic motivational factors and perceived need deficiencies as a function of job level in an urban school district.* Unpublished doctoral dissertation, Memphis State University, Memphis.

Noddings, N. (1992). *The challenge to care in schools*. New York: Teachers College Press.

Okeafor, K. R., & Teddlie, C. (1989). Organizational factors related to administrators' confidence in teachers. *Journal of Research and Development in Education, 22*, 28–36.

Owens, R. G., & Valesky, T. C. (2007). *Organizational behavior in education: Adaptive leadership and school reform*. Boston: Pearson.

Pajak, E., & Blase, J. (1989). The impact of teacher's personal lives on professional role enactment. *American Educational Research Journal, 26*(2), 283–310.

Parks, D. J. (1983). Leadership in times of austerity. *Educational Leadership, 40*(5), 11–13.

Pearson, L. C. & Moomaw, W. (2005). The relationship between teacher autonomy and stress, work satisfaction, empowerment, and professionalism. *Educational Research Quarterly, 29*(1), 37–53.

Peters, T. (1987). *Thriving on chaos: Handbook for a management revolution*. New York: Harper & Row.

Peterson, K. (1978). The principal's tasks. *Administrators' Notebook, 28*(8), 1–4.

Pfeffer, J. (1981). *Power in organizations*. Marshfield, MA: Pitman.

Porter, L. W., Bigley, G. A., & Steers, R. M. (2003). *Motivation and work behavior* (7th ed.). Boston: McGraw-Hill/Irwin.

Purkey, S. C., & Smith, M. S. (1983). Effective schools: A review. *Elementary School Journal, 83*(4), 427–452.

Reiss, F., & Hoy, W. K. (1998). Faculty loyalty: An important but neglected concept in the study of schools. *Journal of School Leadership, 8*, 4–25.

Reitzug, U. C. (1997). Images of principal instructional leadership: From supervision to collaborative inquiry. *Journal of Curriculum and Supervision, 12*(4), 356–366.

Reitzug, U. C., & Cross, B. E. (1994, April). *A multi-site case study of site-based management in urban schools*. Paper presented at the annual meeting of American Educational Research Association, New Orleans, LA.

Richardson, J. (2001). *Seeing through new eyes: Walk-throughs offer new way to view schools*. Oxford, OH: National Staff Development Council.

Rinehart, J. S., Short, P. M., Short, R. J., & Eckley, M. (1998). Teacher empowerment and principal leadership: Understanding the influence process. *Educational Administration Quarterly, 34*, 630–649.

Riordan, G., & da Costa, J. L. (1998, April). *Leadership for effective teacher collaboration: Suggestions for principals and teacher leaders*. Paper presented at the annual meeting of the American Educational Research Association, San Diego, CA.

Rosenblum, S., Louis, K. S., & Rossmiller, R. A. (1994). School leadership and teacher quality of work life in restructuring schools. In J. Murphy & K. S. Louis (Eds.), *Reshaping the principalship: Insights from transformational reform efforts* (pp. 99–122). Thousand Oaks, CA: Corwin Press.

Rosenholtz, S. J. (1989). *Teachers' workplace: The social organization of schools*. New York: Longman.

Rosenholtz, S., & Simpson, C. (1990). Workplace conditions and the rise and fall of teachers' commitment. *Sociology of Education, 63*, 241–257.

Russell, J. S., Mazzarella, J. A., White, T., & Maurer, S. (1985). *Linking the behaviors and activities of secondary school principals to school effectiveness: A focus on effective and ineffective behaviors.* Eugene: University of Oregon, Center for Educational Policy and Management.

Rutter, M., Maugham, B., Mortimore, P., Ouston, J., & Smith, A. (1979). *Fifteen thousand hours: Secondary schools and their effects on children.* Cambridge, MA: Harvard University Press.

Ryan, R. M., & Deci, E. L. (2003). Self-determination theory and the facilitation of intrinsic motivation, social development, and well-being. In L. W. Porter, G. A. Bigley, & R. M. Steers (Eds.), *Motivation and work behavior* (7th ed., pp. 49–65). Boston: McGraw-Hill/Irwin.

Safire, W., & Safir, L. (1990). *Leadership.* New York: Simon & Schuster.

Schein, E. H. (1985). *Organizational culture and leadership.* San Francisco: Jossey-Bass.

Schlechty, P. C. (1990). *Schools for the 21st century.* San Francisco: Jossey-Bass.

Schmuck, R. A. (2006). *Practical action research for change.* Thousand Oaks, CA: Corwin Press.

Schön, D. A. (1983). *The reflective practitioner: How professionals think in action.* New York: Basic Books.

Schön, D. A. (1991). *The reflective turn: Case studies in and on educational practice.* New York: Teachers College Press.

Seligman, M. E. P. (1991). *Learned optimism.* New York: Knopf.

Seligman, M. E. P., Steen, T. A., Park, N., and Peterson, C. (2005). Positive psychology progress: Empirical validation of interventions. *American Psychologist, 60*(5), 410–421.

Sergiovanni, T. J. (1992). *Moral leadership: Getting to the heart of school improvement.* San Francisco: Jossey-Bass.

Sergiovanni, T. (2001). *The principalship: A reflective practice perspective* (4th ed.). Boston: Allyn & Bacon.

Shakeshaft, C. (1987). *Women in educational administration.* Newbury Park, CA: Sage.

Sheldon, S. B. (2003). Linking school-family-community partnerships in urban elementary schools to student achievement on state tests. *The Urban Review, 35*(2), 149–165.

Sheppard, B. (1996). Exploring the transformational nature of instructional leadership. *Alberta Journal of Educational Research, 42*(4), 325–344.

Short, P. (1994). Defining teacher empowerment. *Education, 114*(4), 488–493.

Short, P. M., & Greer, J. T. (1997). *Leadership in empowered schools: Themes from innovative efforts.* Upper Saddle River, NJ: Merrill.

Short, P. M., & Rinehart, J. S. (1992). School participant empowerment scale: Assessment of level of empowerment within the school environment. *Educational and Psychological Measurement, 52*(4), 951–960.

Spector, P. E. (2002). Employee control and occupational stress. *Current Directions in Psychological Science, 11*, 133–136.

Spillane, J. P., Halverson, R., & Diamond, J. B. (2004). Towards a theory of leadership practice: A distributed perspective. *Journal of Curriculum Studies, 36*, 3–34.

Starratt, R. J. (2005). Cultivating the moral character of learning and teaching: A neglected dimension of education. *School Leadership and Management, 25*(4), 399–411.

Stewart, J. (2006). Transformational leadership: An evolving concept examined through the works of Burns, Bass, Avolio, and Leithwood. *Canadian Journal of Educational Administration and Policy, 54*. Retrieved October 17, 2007, from http://www.umanitoba.ca/publications/cjeap/articles/stewart.html

Stogdill, R. (1963). *Manual for the LBDQ-Form 12: An experimental revision.* Columbus: Ohio State University, Bureau of Business Research.

Stone, R. (2004). *Best teaching practices for reaching all learners.* Thousand Oaks, CA: Corwin Press.

Teddlie, C., Falkowski, C., Stringfield, S., Desselle, S., & Garvue, R. (1984). *Louisiana school effectiveness study: Phase two, 1982–84.* Baton Rouge: Louisiana State Department of Education Bureau of Research.

Tesch, R. (1988, April). *The contribution of a qualitative method: Phenomenological research.* Paper presented at the annual meeting of the American Educational Research Association, New Orleans, LA.

Treslan, D. L., & Ryan, J. J. (1986). Perceptions of principals' influence bases. *Canadian Administrator, 26*(2), 1–7.

Tschannen-Moran, M., Hoy, A. W., & Hoy, W. K. (1998). Teacher efficacy: Its meaning and measure. *Review of Educational Research, 68*(2), 204–248.

Uline, C. L., Miller, D. M., & Tschannen-Moran, M. (1998). School effectiveness: The underlying dimensions. *Educational Administration Quarterly, 34*(4), 462–483.

Walberg, H. J., & Haertel, G. D. (Eds.) (1997). *Psychology and educational practice.* Berkeley, CA: McCutchan.

Wang, M. C., Haertel, G. D., & Walberg, H. J. (1993). Toward a knowledge base for school learning. *Review of Educational Research, 63*(3), 249–294.

Ward, M. E. & MacPhail-Wilcox, B. (1999). *Delegation and Empowerment: Leading with and through others.* Larchmont, NY: Eye On Education.

Waters, T., Marzano, R. J., & McNulty, B. A. (2003). *Balanced leadership: What 30 years of research tells us about the effect of leadership on student achievement.* Aurora, CO: Mid-Continent Research for Education and Learning.

Weber, M. (1947). *The theory of social and economic organization.* A.M. Henderson and T. Parsons (Translators). T. Parsons (Ed.) New York: Free Press. (Originally published in 1924.)

Weil, M., Marshalek, B., Mitman, A., Murphy, J., Hallinger, P., & Pruyn, P. (1984, April). *Effective and typical schools: How different are they?* Paper presented at the annual meeting of the American Educational Research Association, New Orleans.

Weiss, C. (1990, April). *How much shared leadership is there in public high schools?* Paper presented at the annual meeting of the American Educational Research Association, Boston, MA.

Willower, D. (1994). *Educational administration: Inquiry, values, practice.* Lancaster, PA: Technomic.

Wimpelberg, R. K., Teddlie, C., & Stringfield, S. (1989). Sensitivity to context: The past and present of effective schools research. *Educational Administration Quarterly, 25*, 82–107.

Wolcott, H. (1973). *The man in the principal's office: An ethnography.* New York: Holt, Rinehart & Winston.

Women's Educational Equity Act Publishing Center. (1990). *Women in school administration.* Newton, MA: Author.

Wong, K. C. (1998). Culture and moral leadership in education. *Peabody Journal of Education*, 73(2), 106–25.

Worthy, J. (2005). It didn't have to be so hard: The first years of teaching in an urban school. *International Journal of Qualitative Studies in Education*, 18(3), 379–398.

Yukl, G. (2006). *Leadership in organizations* (6th ed.). Upper Saddle River, NJ: Pearson Prentice Hall.

Index

NOTE: Entries followed by *n* indicate notes; *t* indicate tables.

**CORWIN
PRESS**

The Corwin Press logo—a raven striding across an open book—represents the union of courage and learning. Corwin Press is committed to improving education for all learners by publishing books and other professional development resources for those serving the field of PreK–12 education. By providing practical, hands-on materials, Corwin Press continues to carry out the promise of its motto: **"Helping Educators Do Their Work Better."**